ESCAPES
FROM THE
NOOSE

ESCAPES
FROM THE
NOOSE

STEPHEN WADE

AMBERLEY

First published 2010

Amberley Publishing Plc
Cirencester Road, Chalford,
Stroud, Gloucestershire, GL6 8PE

www.amberleybooks.com

British Library Cataloguing in Publication Data.
A catalogue record for this book is available from the British Library.

ISBN 978 1 84868 232 0

Typesetting and Origination by FONTHILLDESIGN.
Printed in Great Britain.

Contents

Introduction

In his brief history of the royal pardon published in 1978, C. H. Rolph pointed out that 'the standard law books seem little concerned with the palpably innocent man wrongly convicted.' In 2009, there was a glut of such cases in the national newspapers, mostly because of advances in DNA sampling. There may have been little change in the law books for students in this respect, and so this book has a similar aim to that of Rolph: to give the general reader and the social historian an introduction and a case book, which will highlight the issues and debates around reprieves and pardons in British history since the eighteenth century.

The very words related to this subject resonate with drama and suspense: *pardon, mercy, reprieve, respite* and *commutation*. Perhaps the quickest way to grasp the sensation inherent in these stories is to imagine the scene in the 'hanging committee' around 1800 when the Recorder and other dignitaries would consider the list of the condemned, noting those who had received recommendations from the circuit judges and from the sovereign, and decide on life or death. Similarly, after the creation of the court of criminal appeal in 1907, the trial records are there for any historian with a curiosity about what kinds of topics in those courts led to convictions being quashed. Sometimes it was a legal procedural technicality; or at times it could be new evidence. But the last page of the report in the Sweet and Maxwell volumes indicates the result.

Naturally, when we reflect that capital punishment existed in Britain from the time of the Anglo-Saxons to 1964 (and later than that if we count the states of Jersey and the Isle of Man) the importance of the royal pardon takes prominence. But stays of execution existed in all kinds of forms. Most common through the centuries was 'benefit of clergy' which meant that if a defendant could recite the 'neck verse' – the opening lines of the 51st psalm – then there would be a reprieve. This happened only once, and later the punishment of having the thumb branded as well. If a second capital offence was committed, then the brand would show that this was a second offence and there would be no benefit of clergy.

In the medieval period, and in later Saxon times, there were many kinds of alternatives to a death sentence for felonies, but in the eighteenth century and the Regency, there was a gradual increase in capital offences and so the ritual of public execution (until 1868) was a massively attractive prospect for the media. The potential pardon or reprieve was a very prominent part of that process. For instance, imagine the scene in April, 1836, when Curly Bill Fisher and James Hills, the so-called Chipstead Burglars, were expecting to be executed and were ordered to attend chapel, where the chaplain of St Saviour's, Southwark, was to speak. The cleric at the time chose as his text the fourth verse of the 51st psalm: 'Against thee – thee only have I sinned, and done this evil in they sight.' The criminals were reminded in no uncertain terms that the wages of sin was death.

The Times reported that Fisher, 'the doomed' was conducted to his cell and then visited by the chaplain and those permitted to see him by a magistrate's order. Then we have this paragraph:

'A respite was received from Lord John Russell late on Saturday evening by the sheriff, ordering him to stay the execution of James Hills. We are assured that the respited convict has never implicated himself or Fisher, alias 'Curly Bill' in respect of the murder of Mr Richardson of Banstead.'

The report concludes with words which were repeated time and again through the dark years of execution in this country: 'The apparatus of death was erected on the lodge of the prison on Saturday and during the whole of yesterday the area opposite was crowded with spectators ...'

The word 'respite' simply meant a discharge, and came from the Home Office (created in 1782) and so the vocabulary of 'escapes from the noose' needs to be clarified now:

Commutation: The change of a sentence from a severe to a less severe one.

Mercy: Clemency and compassion, linked to the royal pardon as far back as the reign of Edward the Confessor (1042-1066) when the king used the royal prerogative of mercy to an offender by mitigating or removing the consequences of conviction.

Pardon: Release from an offence by the crown.

Reprieve: The suspension of the execution of a sentence. In the context of this book this means the Home Secretary acting with the prerogative of mercy in place of the crown.

Respite: A discharge.

Basically, this vocabulary was applied in a variety of contexts, and the concepts were taken up by writers, statesmen and philosophers as the centuries wore on, so that built into the criminal justice system was a network of potential actions of clemency. The assize judges from the beginnings of those courts in the twelfth century made recommendations and even in the years between *c.* 1770 and 1820, when the number of capital crimes moved from a hundred to over two hundred, the recommendations to mercy were at a high level. Between 1800 and 1834 for instance, there were 29,808 sentences of death and of these people only 2,676 were hanged. By the last years of the nineteenth century the rate of execution for murderers after sentencing was 54 per cent, 46 per cent of these being reprieved between 1865 and 1899.

This book recounts the development of reprieves over the centuries, and in that story there are significant milestones, so that in spite of the numerous murder acts of the mid to late eighteenth century, it has to be said that the Home Office and the judge's clemency was still marked. Many death sentences were commuted to transportation in the period after 1787 for example, when Tasmania and Australia were opened up as penal settlements, and many convicts were sent to the hulks, the notorious prison ships, in the Thames estuary.

The cases I have selected, from many thousands of such narratives, represent a range of aspects of the subject, and what they are really concerned with are the destinations of the convicts concerned. By that I mean the alternatives to the noose: transportation, the asylum, life imprisonment and of course, acquittal. They account for most but, of course, we have to factor in the advent of suicide also: some 'destinations' away from state executions led to self-murder.

There is not a great deal available on this aspect of criminal history, but I owe thanks to two writers in particular: Fenton Bresler and C. H. Rolph. Bresler's *Reprieve, The Study of a System* (1965) and Rolph's *The Queen's Pardon* (1978) are extremely valuable groundbreakers in this area of interest. See the bibliography for full details. Bresler gave a full history of the notion of 'reprieve' and used very prominent cases from the twentieth century. Here, I extend that into some by-ways so that we may enlighten and broaden the whole spectrum, from the sad stories of diminished responsibility to the complex courtroom dramas.

Of course, some pardons have been posthumous, notably those given to Timothy Evans and to David Bentley. But there is the other side to the story in miscarriages of justice. In recent years, the Criminal Cases Review Commission has been prominent (and over-worked) in this respect. But in some of my chosen cases, there are clearly some cases in this category, and what strikes the modern reader when reflecting on the situation in the courts before the appearance of the court of criminal appeal in 1907, is just how little there was for the poor labouring person who stood accused.

What did exist before 1907 was for a minority – the 'Court for Crown Cases Reserved.' These records were published by Cox in the 1840s and are arranged in print by circuits. This court was very old, going back to the medieval years. It was a kind of appeal court, but only for assize cases and it had the power to respite an execution or to postpone a judgement. What would happen here was that a judge would call this meeting in order to take the advice and opinions of his learned colleagues. In other words, the appeals came from judges only, and were often on points of law. If the group of learned judges thought that a person was innocent after this deliberation, then they had the power to give a pardon.

In 1848, the institution became formally acknowledged by the Indictable Offences Act, and this defined the Crown Cases Reserved as a tribunal composed of five judges, and one of these had to be the Lord Chief Justice. If there was no agreement on a matter, then a larger assembly in court of fifteen judges could be called.

As a coda to the general assumption in what has been said so far, that Britain had a heartless penchant for hangings and that there was perhaps no direct channel to the highest courts for mercy, then it should be mentioned that the House of Lords also had a part to play. In the House of Lords Journal for 1645 we have a plea for pardon regarding a group of prisoners in Northampton. The petition was from the justices of the peace, and they wrote: '*We whose names are subscribed … do humbly desire that a pardon may be granted unto Thomas Cleaver, John Appleyard, Blaze Adams, condemned for horse-stealing; for Robert Linacre and Edward Ward, condemned for murdering a woman, tying her in the water for witchcraft; for Alice Hampton a cut-purse, and Elizabeth Warwick for murder, both old reprieves, condemned many years since: all of which prisoners are now lying in great misery in the gaol at Northampton, to the extreme charge of the country …*'

It is interesting to note the reasons: 'misery' and the cost of keeping them incarcerated. They had been sentenced to lie in gaol with no determined length of stay, and something desperate had to be done. The Lords replied with a pardon:

'Ordered, by the Lords and Commons assembled in Parliament, that Mr Solicitor General draw a pardon, and that the Commissioners of the Great Seal do pass the same under the Broad Seal, to such convicted prisoners in the gaol at Northampton, which are certified by the justices of the peace for the county in their certificates hereunto annexed ...'

In effect, the local justices had brought into action the Lord Chancellor, who had the Great Seal in his care and used that to issue the required writ; also they involved the Solicitor General, the Attorney General's deputy. There was clearly a great deal of cash to be saved in releasing the prisoners, and the plea for a pardon had nothing to do with wanting to claim any miscarriage of justice or similar matters. It was purely an economic transaction, although the justices had stated their feeling of compassion for the suffering of the convicts. It is worth recalling that the local gaols at that time were places with a high death-rate due to the execrable insanitary conditions.

In more recent times, popular feeling expressed in a petition might have much the same effect, as in this press announcement from 1934:

'*Horace Wiggan, 25, the Barnsley miner who was recently sentenced to death for the murder of Mrs Ada Perkins, with whom he had lived, has been reprieved and the sentence commuted to one of penal servitude for life. Last week a petition, signed by over 42,000 people, asking for Wiggan's reprieve, was presented ...*'

The aim here, then, is to give an account of the range of cases which, for various reasons, demonstrate the permutations of reprieve and pardon in our criminal law through history.

Acknowledgements

In preparing and researching this book, obviously I have needed a great deal of help. Librarians and archivists have been most helpful, in particular staff at the East Riding Archives and at Doncaster Archives; material from the *Yorkshire Post* archives has been helpful, and naturally, editors at Amberley have played an important part too. Although some of these stories have been covered more sketchily in previous books, it has to be stressed that there has been new work done by historians and true crime writers. This is the case with the Madeleine Smith story, and the recent work by Jimmy Powdrell Campbell has been most useful.

Help and support also comes in conversations and letters of course, so thanks go to Brian Elliott and to Kate Walker in particular.

For some illustrations, my appreciation goes to Vicki Schofield.

Pardons from Medieval to Tudor

The notion of a royal pardon between the accession of William I and the Tudors was largely something concerned with power rather than with mercy. We like to think that a pardon is some kind of honourable, humane measure taken against a transgressor, and that, as Shakespeare famously said, 'The quality of mercy is not strained.' But in fact, after the Anglo-Saxon and Roman years in Britain, when laws had developed in certain regions in which various Saxon kings had worked out a *wergild* – a 'worth money' for crimes – the pardon became a concept that would, on the one hand increase the prestige and status of a monarch, and on the other hand provide a touch of 'PR' as mercy was shown openly and with great pomp and ceremony.

We must first consider the partner of the pardon and the reprieve – capital punishment. In the Saxon centuries, there was hanging as a standard punishment for such offences as murder and cowardice, but there was also a variety of other punishments. But to take a man's life was as often related to religious and moral concepts as much as to a strict criminal code. In the Medieval period, outlawry was a common option in the courts, but that really meant a death penalty, as the culprit would be hounded and hunted down, killed, and all his property taken from him. The old phrase relating to this is far from the world of Robin Hood – the outlaw should be treated 'like the head of a wolf.'

In the earliest times of Celtic Britain, the tribes existing before the Roman conquest clearly had capital punishment, but with the Saxons, the concept of punishment, tied to the *wergild*, meant that there was a sliding scale, so that the notion of *manbot* was created: this referred to slaves, so that a slave had value. The *wergild* and the *manbot* meant that, for instance, the money paid in compensation for a tooth being knocked out was one shilling in *c.* 600, according to the laws of Ethelbert of Kent. If a person could not pay the *bot*, the results were dire. It was possible that the offender could lose all his land, or be outlawed, or even be ordered to pay something to the King; a fine called a *wite*.

There is no mercy in any of this; merely a money motive and an eye to profit in actions of grievous bodily harm. It took changes in the nature of kingship to bring about developments in the criminal justice system of course, and before the creation of a national state around 900 AD. Therefore King Edward the Elder's reign saw the beginnings of more definite engagement with the justice system from the sovereign. In the middle years of the tenth century Edward ruled that if someone forced their way into another person's home then that transgressor was breaking the custom of royal protection. That offender would be deemed to be *botleas* – having no status to provide compensation. The result was that it was the King's decision regarding what would happen to that offender; whether he would live or die, in effect.

Not long before the Norman Conquest, then, the status of the King as someone who could act by giving a pardon was established; although death by hanging would be the obvious result, the King could also elect to substitute other forms of punishment such as maiming and mutilation or even drowning or stoning. Perhaps the most astonishing and impressive document in this context before 1066 is a law of King Cnut of 1023 with the following decrees:

> 'If anyone eagerly wishes to turn from wrongdoing back to right behaviour, one is to be merciful to him very readily, as best one can, for the fear of God. And let us always help quickest those who need it most. The weak man must always be judged and prescribed for more leniently than the strong, for the love of God. For we know full well that the feeble cannot bear a burden like the strong ... For we know that we must moderate and distinguish reasonably between age and youth, wealth and poverty, freedom and slavery, health and sickness ... Also in many a deed when a man acts under compulsion, he is then more entitled to clemency in that he did what he did out of necessity ... and if anyone acts unintentionally, he is not entirely like one who does it intentionally ...'

The last sentence and the one previous to that contain the kernel of all the major issues concerning pardons in the medieval centuries. At the centre was the problem of what to do about the unintentional slayer. A cursory glance at the court records of manors and bishoprics over the thirteenth century, for instance, makes it clear that those with ecclesiastical power and those with the administration of the eyre – the circuit court established in 1176 who were supposed (by the Magna Carta) to go into every county once every year – could hang felons at their local gallows. Publications of county records societies today show thousands of cases of forced entry, assault, murder and rape for which there was merely a fine or an acquittal. Therefore, it is clear that Cnut was ahead of his time, but later, with the reforms of the fourteenth century and the creation of assize courts, the king emerged as an entity linked profoundly with the notion of a pardon.

Even in the fourteenth century there was no dependable outcome of a trial. A general issue of a pardon could be done if the king needed soldiers; the offender could go and fight on campaign; sometimes the king needed money and would therefore benefit from a large fine rather than having a man hanged. There was no financial benefit in giving a royal pardon. By the reign of Henry I hanging was generally established, after his father, William the Conqueror, had decreed that 'no-one would be killed or hanged for any cause.' Henry's reign saw such events as the mass hanging in 1124 of 44 thieves in Leicestershire; death at that time was the punishment for treason, burglary, arson, robbery, theft and homicide.

The contrast between the Anglo-Saxon world and the later medieval years then is seen in this contrast: in the seventh century under Ethelbert, a murderer might pay a hundred shillings, but for grievous bodily harm the wergild was only twenty shillings. There was compensation demanded by the church courts as well; for instance, if offences were committed on holy days. In other words, the Saxon saw offences as transgressions against the community and saw reparation in terms of wealth. By c. 1100, there was more chance of a hanging and so there were more appeals for pardon.

Clearly, before the later kings' reigns, in which the assizes began to have more power, the situation was one in which the local power-base had immense control and influence; that is to say, the church and the manor. When justices of the peace were created in 1361, there was a markedly more streamlined approach to the administration of justice and offenders and more notice taken of gaols and the need for gaol delivery at certain times of the year. In most cases, the early medieval prisons of local barons were places where one could expect to languish and then die before a court appearance occurred.

In the centuries before the assizes, established in the reign of Henry II, and the beginnings of the idea of the grand jury in the 1166 Assize of Clarendon, the barbarity in penal thinking was clearly a deterrent to the seasoned villain and a horror for the everyday citizen who found himself in trouble with the law. A man with no legal process behind him would stand with his accuser and there would be an ordeal; this could be the ordeal of cold water, hot water or of fire. In the first of these, the accused was tied and thrown into deep water, and if he sank he was classified as innocent; in the second, the accused had to put his hand into boiling water to grasp a stone, and if his hand had healed three days later he was cleared of the charge; in the final ordeal of fire, the accused had to hold a hot iron bar and keep hold as he took nine paces, and again, healing had to take place in three days for him to be cleared.

To summarise all this criminal justice chaos in the centuries before the Tudors, there was always uncertainty at trial; outlawry and fines were common, as were acquittals, but if a punishment was given, the consequences were never anticipated as if there was a codification of sentences and a regular ruling. For instance, in a case from 1282 from the Yorkshire eyre, there were four prisoners who had been gaoled in 1279; then, after three years in prison, two men were judged to have killed by accident and were released and then pardoned; the two others who had clearly killed in self-defence were never pardoned.

In countless cases of homicide in the medieval centuries, there is evidence of confusion and miscarriage of justice in all areas; a story that illustrates this is from 1290 in which John de Oklesthorp was bailed after a verdict of killing in self defence. What happened was that John and his friend Hugh were bailiffs and had seized a cart and horse from Robert Turpin, who had followed them wielding an axe, and had been shot with an arrow by John; as the bailiffs then grappled with Robert, the arrow was forced deeper into his chest and he died. The evidence showed that John pushed the arrows into the chest (and he had fired the shot). Yet John was pardoned and Hugh was hanged. There is no sound reason why John was pardoned.

But nevertheless, in the twelfth and thirteenth centuries there were all kinds of measures taken to reform and modernise the penal and criminal justice system; specialist historians of the subject of pardons have demonstrated effectively that royal pardons were created to play a principal part in these reforms. But Cnut's wise words about killings done 'unintentionally' were never going to be clear-cut in the courts, and those who might be termed 'excusable slayers' would never have been confident of a fair outcome after legal process in these years. The prospect of serving the King against the Scots or the Irish must have seemed much brighter than outlawry or taking your chance in a court.

In the Tudor period, the nature of the royal pardon was to change radically. Although on the surface, and with the images of popular culture in mind, the Tudor dynasty appears to be one of mass slaughter sanctioned by the sovereign and state, there is ample evidence that the royal pardon really came into its own in this century. Cynthia Herrup's influential book, *The Common Peace* (1987) has shown that pardons were used with a sense of realpolitick and pragmatism, being part of a process of creating the kinds of citizens the Tudor enterprise wanted – people who could be formed and moulded into subservience.

Anyone in Tudor Britain must have been aware how easy it was to slip into a category of behaviour which could be termed 'treasonable.' Historians of the period have often pointed out the similarity between Tudor policy and the Soviet oppression under Stalin. A trial for treason was the surest way for the state to bring down anyone who was deemed to be unacceptable in beliefs or actions. One foreign visitor to England in 1558, Etienne Perlin, in *Description des Royaulmes D'Angleterre*, noted that 'a man cannot be certain from one day to the next who might be closest to the King's confidence and who degraded, stripped of his possessions and imprisoned awaiting the death of a traitor.' Perhaps the defining statute in this respect was that of 1534, a Treason Act elaborating on the old, basic definition of treason as 'compassing or imagining the King's death' and 'levying war against the King in his realm' or 'adhering to the King's enemies in his realm, giving them aid and comfort here and elsewhere' (Treason Act 1351). The 1534 Act added the words, 'Those who maliciously wish, will or desire, by words or writing, or by craft imagine the King's death.'

Bearing in mind the frequent uprisings and revolts of the sixteenth century, notably the 1536 Pilgrimage of Grace and the 1569 rising of the Northern Earls, it is plain to see why there was so much repression. Clearly, the religious ferment made matters worse, and there is paranoia in much of Henry VIII's actions of repression, and again with Elizabeth's tough actions on plotters. But the state was so extreme and terrifying that a man who wrote to Lady Lisle in 1535 could say, 'It is rumoured that a person should be committed to the Tower for saying that this month will be rainy and full of wet, next month death and the third, war.'

In this context, as Cynthia Herrup has shown, the royal pardon was such a stunningly effective public relations exercise that the Tudor monarchs, mostly experts in 'spin,' cultivated its use. She notes that Henry VIII for instance, issued five general pardons in his reign, and over 1,600 people were saved. The patent rolls for 1485-1603, covering the whole dynasty, show almost 14,000 people who were given grants of mercy. Herrup has made a convincing case for the view that the Tudors saw the value in demonstrating mercy as a way to persuade people that a trial was to be preferred to outlawry. After all, this was the age of the 'sturdy beggar' and the massive problems of the parish labour troubles, when legislation on apprentices, masters and servants, and poor houses was created. It was also the age which made the house of correction. In short, there was repression, but there was also a clever dissemination of an ideology that gave a semblance of a beneficent state and an enlightened monarch. Although Henry VIII was the man who promised pardon to the leaders of the Pilgrimage of Grace and then saw dozens of them hanged both in London and in the north, he was also the man who revelled in demonstrating his capacity for mercy.

Mary was the same. In the aftermath of the Wyatt revolt, she showed the same public image. Sir Thomas Wyatt was a poet and courtier, and he had land in Kent. When Queen Mary was to marry Philip of Spain, it was all too much for him and later he took part in what he thought was a general revolt across the land, but in effect it was merely a Kent uprising. He failed and was hanged on Tower Hill in April, 1554. On that occasion, over four hundred of Wyatt's followers were brought from Kent to the London prisons, strapped together like animals going to the slaughter; but in the courtyard at Westminster they all knelt and begged for mercy. Queen Mary graciously gave her pardon.

It has been estimated that in Henry VIII's reign, 72,000 people were executed. But again, it was clear from early in his reign that if there were to be pardons, then he would have the monopoly. In a statute of 1536 we have these words:

'No person or persons of what estate or degree so ever they be of shall have any power or auctorities to pardon or remit any treasons, murders, manslaughters or any kyndes of felonyes … but that the Kings highness, his heirs and successors … Kings of this realm shall have the whole and sole power and auctorities thereof united and knytte to the imperiall Crown of the realm…'

In this same period, the famous lawyer Sir Edward Coke stated that the pardon only applied to public offences which had been prosecuted by the crown. He also said that the royal pardon could negate the death penalty, but the King could not change the form of the execution. This was important because the different methods of execution given to people of different rank or whose crimes were in law to be punished by a specific form of execution had to relate to the written law, and the sovereign could not interfere with such procedures.

Paradoxically then, the Tudors learned the value of a pardon as a powerful tool to promote conformity and adherence to the state. There could be as many secret executions as a sovereign desired, but if pardons were public, then they would have the attention of the London mob and the word would be passed around that the King or Queen was munificent and a good Christian prince. The iconic words were created: '*Now know ye that We in consideration of some circumstances humbly represented to Us, are graciously pleased to extend Our Grace and Mercy unto the said……*'

There were also the more routine pardons and reprieves in the Tudor courts, notably the concept of the 'pleading the belly' appeal in court. The thinking here was the chid in the womb could not be considered guilty and so should not hang. The notion was that the reprieve was temporary, the mother supposedly being hanged after the birth of the child. But, as James Sharpe has shown in his book, *Crime In Early Modern England*, it was common for these mothers to be fully pardoned. He points out that in the Home circuit of assizes between 1558 and 1625, 'nearly half of the women convicted of a felony claimed to be pregnant and over a third (38%) were successful in their claim.' The procedure was that a group of matrons would examine the woman in court who claimed to be pregnant; these were wives and midwives, arbiters of the female body, and of course, they would have a whole panoply of various bits of knowledge with which to examine the women.

Pardon in Tudor England was, of course, also related to people with wealth and a certain 'high degree' – the everyday villain or rogue would end with a date on the scaffold or languish forgotten in a hellish prison. The only other possibility of a reprieve would come from the 'benefit of clergy' as discussed in the introduction.

Between the Tudors and the arrival of the Hanoverians in the eighteenth century, little changed in this context; the escapes from the rope open to felons consisted of pardons, benefit of clergy or 'pleading the belly.' But generally the hangman was busy; the sixteenth to eighteenth centuries, before the creation of the Home Office and the Home Secretary, were years of savagery in the criminal justice system. Throughout the Georgian period, various murder acts created more and more capital crimes.

In terms of pardons and reprieves the watershed came in 1782 when the Home Office became central to the whole business of reprieves and respites.

2

The Beginnings of the Home Office

One of the most heart-rending experiences in family history research is to look through the pardoning archive at The National Archives and read the desperate pleas to the Home Secretary from relatives and friends, seeking the pardon of their convicted friend or family member. These letters are either asking for a life to be spared or for a commutation of a sentence. Such measures were the only option for ordinary people until the Court of Criminal Appeal was established in 1907. The letters were to the Home Office from 1782 because from that date, when the Office was formed, the pleas were to the Home Secretary and not to the sovereign.

At the assizes, the courts held in major towns on the assize circuits across the land, the judges had the power, after a sentence of death, to issue a certificate of pardon, but these were simply recommendations. They went to the Home Office and the result might be a free pardon, a commutation of sentence to prison, or to transportation. The process of pardon could also include additional statements made by any person of status and influence which might back up the appeal.

At the Home Office, there would then be a meeting, and a Recorder's report would issue the decisions. Of course, the King could still be involved and there were clashes between the King and the Home Secretaries at times.

The Home Office was formed in 1782 after radical parliamentary structural changes. There had been two departments of state for hundreds of years, one for the Northern Department (dealing with Europe) and one for the Southern Department (dealing with France and the colonies). These were both foreign offices, of course. The secretary handling affairs at home was of no real consequence; but then, Charles James Fox began the move to create what became the Home Office, a responsibility for home and colonial business.

In terms of law and the criminal justice system, for centuries the structure had been that each county had a Lord Lieutenant and a Sheriff, with the magistrates acting with them. For instance, these persons were present at a hanging; the specific order of the ritual walk to the scaffold involved the Lord Lieutenant and Sheriff as well as the prisoner governor, the priest, doctor and hangman. But from 1782, there would be a Home Secretary and he would be the person at the head of the criminal justice system. The Earl of Shelburne became the first man to take that post.

The Recorder's Report came from what became known as the 'Hanging Cabinet.' Various dignitaries would sit and deliberate on the fate of the listed felons from the assize recommendations. The report would then go to the Privy Council and from there matters would reach the executive stage and things would happen. There were mistakes; in 1833, there was a list of respited prisoners sent in the report, and there was just one name omitted from the pardons: Job Cox, who had stolen £5 from a letter. The names were printed in the national newspapers, and there was the name of Job Cox, who was

[484]

T A B L E   V.

An ACCOUNT of the Number of Criminals Condemned to Death; Executed; and Sentenced to Transportation: with their respective Offences: from the Year 1750 to 1772 Inclusive; within the several Counties &c. in the NORFOLK CIRCUIT.

Years.	Petty Treason and Murder.	Burglary and House-breaking.	Robbery in Highway & Dwelling.	Horse-stealing, &c.	Forgery.	Returning from Transportation.	Six other Crimes.	Condemned to Death.	Executed.	Reprieved for Transportation.	Grand Larceny.	Petty Larceny.	Seven other Crimes.	Sentenced to Transportation.
1750	2	3	8	8	--	--	--	21	10	8	24	3	--	35
1751	--	6	4	6	--	--	--	16	12	12	24	--	--	36
1752	3	3	3	15	1	--	3	28	11	13	28	1	2	44
1753	2	4	2	11	--	--	2	21	6	10	18	1	--	29
1754	--	9	2	17	1	--	4	33	13	20	29	1	4	54
1755	--	2	4	7	--	--	1	14	2	9	20	1	1	31
1756	--	2	2	7	--	--	6	17	1	16	18	1	--	36
1757	1	8	5	11	--	--	2	27	6	12	34	--	1	46
1758	--	2	6	15	--	--	1	24	5	23	31	1	2	57
1759	--	2	3	8	--	--	--	13	3	15	12	2	--	29
1760	--	5	3	3	--	--	--	11	3	11	15	--	1	27
1761	1	1	2	2	--	--	2	8	2	4	13	--	1	18
1762	1	1	1	1	2	1	1	8	2	3	10	--	--	15
1763	3	3	1	5	--	--	1	13	5	6	19	1	2	27
1764	--	4	2	8	--	3	2	19	3	10	16	1	4	29
1765	--	4	2	14	--	--	--	20	1	19	29	1	2	52
1766	2	8	4	14	--	--	2	30	4	17	27	--	1	45
1767	2	6	2	14	--	--	6	30	5	38	34	--	--	72
1768	--	1	1	10	--	--	4	16	5	16	35	1	2	55
1769	2	9	1	4	--	1	1	18	6	11	22	--	2	34
1770	--	5	5	12	--	1	1	24	7	17	18	--	--	35
1771	1	4	1	6	--	--	4	16	5	11	30	--	2	43
1772	--	1	1	4	--	--	1	7	--	7	17	--	1	25
Total	20	93	65	202	4	6	44	434	117	308	523	15	28	874

TABLE

Some facts and figures on numbers hanged.

to hang. He was awaiting his fate in Newgate prison when Sir Thomas Denman, the Lord Chief Justice of the King's Bench, saw the list of names; he thought it was simply an error caused by a press reporter working too hastily, and luckily for the condemned man, Denman mentioned this to the under-sheriff, who said that the list was right and that the authorities at Newgate had been told to prepare the man for the scaffold. *The Times* reported the exciting and dramatic consequences of that conversation between lawyers:

> '"What!" said Sir Thomas Denman, "Cox ordered for execution ... Impossible! I was myself one of the Privy Council when the report was made, and I know that no warrant for the execution of anyone was issued. Cox was ordered to be placed in solitary confinement and to be kept to hard labour, previously to his being transported for life, to which punishment the judgement to die was commuted." The under sheriff was very glad to be the bearer of good tidings at Newgate ...'

The reporter explained for the public the nature of the recorder's report: 'It does not consist of a transcript of the shorthand-writer's notes of every particular case, but is merely the condensed account of each case made by the Recorder himself from the shorthand-writer's notes. It is of course liable to some objection ...' That was the understatement of the year for poor Cox.

The recorder's report was a matter of great public interest; in 1820, while the King was at Brighton and there had been a high profile trial of a murder of a gamekeeper at York, clearly the newspapers had to tell the readers who followed the trial that the fate of the killer was in the hands of the Hanging Cabinet. *The Times* reported simply that, 'The King is expected from Brighton tomorrow to receive the Recorder's report.'

Much may be learned about the office of the Home Secretary and the nature of this system when we consider Sir Robert Peel. In January, 1822, Peel became Home Secretary, and he was to be in that office for eight years. In the early phase of Peel's first stint, George IV was involved in pleas for pardon, and began writing to Peel with his recommendations. That was to be the beginning of a series of clashes on matters of reprieve which were to consolidate the status of the Home Secretary in this context. Typical of this confrontation between minister and monarch was the case of a man called Mills. He had been sentenced to death for uttering false notes (counterfeiting) and Lady Conyngham, the mistress of George IV, pressed the King to write to Peel on the matter, wanting a pardon. Peel had decided that there would be no reprieve and he did not give in; he confided to a secretary that if the King insisted, then he would issue a reprieve and then resign from the office. The King gave in on the matter. Mills was hanged.

This continued for some time, with George trying all kinds of methods to insist, sulk or reprimand his Home Secretary. It is easy to imagine the meeting of the Hanging Cabinet – something that George could influence, of course. The King and his ministers and secretaries would comment on the list, no doubt being perfunctory for most cases, but when well-known names occurred – aristocrats, for instance – there would have been some strategies and mind-games between sovereign and servant. But it has been noted by the writer and historian Fenton Bresler that Peel was not necessarily a minister who generally saved the majority of those cases which prompted debate. Bresler wrote that, '... the nation's jurors probably saved more condemned persons' lives than he did.

Peel's personality in these matters, under pressure from above, is perhaps best seen in the forgery case of Peter Comyn, a man who had forged documents and committed arson as an act of vengeance; once again, the King's mistress applied pressure on the King and he did not even use the proper process of law; the King simply wrote to the Lord Lieutenant of Ireland, telling him that he was pardoning Comyn. Peel was furious, naturally. George was near death and on his death-bed when Peel's letter refusing to comply with the pardon reached him. Comyn was hanged, and shortly after, on June 26, 1830, the King died.

Within this general system, it has to be said that matters became complicated and sometimes felons would not take the reprieve. One famous occasion on which the prisoners did not accept the escape from the noose was in 1789, on 19 September. On that day, there were ninety-five capital respites – felons waiting to hear the result of the Recorder's decision. The first fourteen of these people went into the Old Bailey, and after the first man had accepted his reprieve, two men, William Davis and William Rayner, were told of a conditional pardon – transportation for life instead of hanging. Davis said, 'Death is more welcome to me than this pardon!'

Historian Simon Devereaux has explored the possible reasons for this refusal to accept life (changed later). The potential reasons for this odd behaviour throw light on the importance of pardons at the time, when the Home Office was new, of course. Devereaux lists these possible reasons: revolutionary principles; refusal because they thought the King irrelevant (after the French Revolution); death was preferred to life in Van Dieman's Land, or that they wanted to 'die game' as the saying was at the time. That meant that they wanted to put on a show for the mob, as hangings were public then (this being abolished in 1868). They may also have wanted to defy the justice system. All these reasons make sense, and show that the notion of a pardon then was still part of a certain ideology of control, as it had been for the Tudors.

Until 1837, the monarch had the power of life and death over his or her subjects. After that date, the Home Secretary assumed the role of the monarch and gave the royal prerogative of mercy. Clearly, the Hanging Cabinet was generally humane: between 1800 and 1834 for instance, there were 29,808 death sentences and of these, 27,132 were reprieved. When it is recalled that up to the late 1820s there were over two hundred capital offences on the statute books, it locates the 'quality of mercy' strongly in both the work of the judges at assizes and in the Privy Council. The first two decades of the nineteenth century were years of paranoid fear on behalf of the state, after the revolution in France; laws against treason, sedition, taking illegal oaths and the formation of radical political societies were extreme and severe. In 1799 and 1800, the Combination Acts had made gatherings of people in groups of more than six a criminal offence. In Manchester the Peterloo Massacre of 1819 had shown this governmental fear; eleven ordinary people were killed and hundreds wounded as the yeomanry attacked the crowd who were listening to Henry Hunt speak.

With the availability of Tasmania and Australia as convict settlements from the 1780s, it became possible for the authorities to transport the worst criminals away across the oceans rather than hang them all, so some of the pleas for pardon would not have been difficult decisions – out of sight, as opposed to out of life, was the decision.

With Peel, the Home Office had arrived and its power was supreme, a major player in the higher echelons of British justice, the minister sitting with the highest lawyers to decide on the fate of sentenced felons.

Of course, there is more to the mechanisms of 'escapes from the noose' than institutions. Throughout the nineteenth century, the definition of insanity as a defence and of provocation experienced radical change. Reprieves were steadily to involve considerations of mental illness and diminished responsibility. The formative event here is the attempted assassination of Robert Peel's secretary by Daniel McNaghten in 1843. Lord Chief Justice Tindal put the point to the jury that McNaghten had no ability to distinguish between right and wrong because he was insane. In some ways, this is one of the most significant 'escapes' because it gave rise to the McNaghten rules, thought-governing insanity defences for any decades to come. The ruling was that every man is to be presumed sane until the contrary is proved, and that McNaghten was incapable of judging between right and wrong; with regard to the act he now stands accused. They were the best rules available for use in court until they were challenged in the Royal Commission on Capital Punishment of 1949-1953.

This was a very long way from the earlier times, when a life could be 'bought' – as in the case of a young man in 1684 accused of homicide. Gilbert Burnet wrote about this in his classic work, *A History of My Own Times* (1723) and he says that the young man pleaded guilty to murder after the assurance that a pardon could be bought from James II for £16,000. Burnet wrote: '... of which the king had one half and the other half was divided among the two ladies then most in favour.'

In contrast, as the Victorian years rolled on, the accused had increasingly more on his or her side in court with regard to defining murder, and the formative legislation affecting the reduction of capital crimes was the Offences Against the Person Act of 1861, which defined just four capital offences – murder, high treason, piracy and arson in a royal dockyard. Even as early as 1848, the statistics in *The Times* for June, 1849, state that: 'Of the sixty persons sentenced to death in 1848, only 12 were executed – 10 males and 2 females. The offence was, in every case, murder of the most atrocious kind; the motives being principally revenge and jealousy.' The range of offences for which death sentences had been given in that year included malicious wounding, rape, sodomy, burglary and arson.

As will be seen in many of the following crime stories, the Victorians and Edwardians, in particular, were destined to experience the high drama and psychological complications of the insanity and provocation defences, and as forensic science advanced and the appeal court appeared, there would be much less room for manoeuvre in the situation of the person accused of a capital offence and much more potential for the performance skills of the advocates. The task of deciding on reprieves before the 1907 appeal courts was still in the hands of the Home Secretary and the sovereign of course, but there was much less work to do in this respect and the cases that did come up for consideration were very extreme indeed and were almost always murder cases.

3

Lord Santry 1739

In eighteenth century Dublin, the Hell-Fire club met at Daly's club on College Green, and other places rather more in keeping with the Hell-Fire traditions. These were basically organisations which were formed by the bored and rakish sons of the aristocracy, often in old ruins or halls on country estates; they were places where immorality of various kinds could be indulged and practised. They also had ritualistic tendencies, often involving sexual and drunken orgies.

In Dublin, the Hell-Fire club acquired the local name of 'The Devil's Kitchen' and the rascals associated with it were known as 'bucks.' The club was founded by Richard Parsons, Earl of Rosse and Colonel Jack St Leger. These characters were out for a good time and with no sense of restraint. Their motto was 'do as you will.' The wildness of their parties may be illustrated by the tale of Buck Sheely, a man who was caught cheating at cards; after a mock trial, the victim was thrown through the window on the third floor, and he was dressed up as a bull, with actual skin and horns used. It was no joke though, as Sheely died.

In the 1730s in Dublin, a leading group of these rogues was painted by James Worsdale, and his work is in the Irish National Gallery; it shows Lord Santry, Simon Luttrell (the Earl of Carhampton), the colonels Clements, Ponsonby and St George. When this picture was done, Santry was a young rake in his twenties and, as with so many of his peers, he had a penchant for a good, exciting duel. As historian Geoffrey Ashe has written, 'Santry himself notched the barrel of his pistol to mark each deed of blood.'

But Santry was to become an infamous figure in criminal history in 1739, because his mad antics went too far on one occasion, and he took a life – that of footman Laughlin Murphy. The official account of the trial, which took place at the Dublin House of Commons, contains a huge amount of pomp and circumstance; after all, the lords were trying one of their own. Santry was Henry Barry. He had succeeded to the title of the fourth Lord Santry in January, 1735.

The occasion of the trial (27 April) was highly militaristic as well as being colourful and solemn as such major trials were at the time; there was a regiment of infantry on College Green and also a company of battle-axe guards along the road to parliament House. Santry was twenty-nine, and he was taken very early to the court. Waiting for him were the panel of judges and the Lord High Steward. A manuscript written about the event describes the opening of the proceedings:

'The proclamation was made, that the person or persons to whom any writ or precept had been directed, for the certifying any indictment or record before The Lord High Steward, should certify and bring in the same forthwith …

> Whereupon the writ of certiori, with the precept to the Lord Chief Justice ... were delivered in at the table and read by the Clerk of the Crown of the King's bench, whereupon the sheriffs of the city of Dublin gave in the writ for bringing up the prisoner ...'

This has all the tenor and import of something heavily serious, indicating that there was something momentous about the fact that a rake and a Hell-Fire member had been brought to justice. Santry was then brought to the bar; he made three reverences and a salute was returned. Clearly, here was no ordinary trial of a petty criminal.

The crime had allegedly been committed in a public house in Palmerstown on the 9 August in the previous year; Santry and his bucks were in a room in the tavern enjoying themselves and Murphy was in a kitchen, linked to the room by a narrow corridor. Murphy was employed as a general servant really, doing such things as carrying messages, being a porter and helping in travel arrangements. He was a married man and had three children, and as the Attorney General at the trial made a point of saying that poor Murphy was 'a person who with a good deal of industry and difficulty maintained himself and family...'

After the main celebrations of the evening had passed and most guests had left, an argument developed between Santry and a man called Humphreys. Everyone was intoxicated, as witnesses said; a certain witness, Jocelyn, testified that Santry had twice tried to draw his sword to set about attacking Humphreys that night.

Santry raged out down the passage to the kitchen and there he bumped into Murphy. He shoved him away and shouted that he would kill the next man who said a word. For some reason, Murphy did speak, and they were his last words. The drunken Santry, totally out of control, stabbed his servant and mortally wounded him. But he was a long time dying. On the night of the stabbing, so the writer of the trial report said,

> 'The poor man spoke, and the noble Lord the prisoner too punctually performed what he had so rashly sworn and stabbed him. Upon this the man went into a room near the kitchen, stayed but a little while, and came back into the kitchen; the blood gushed out of the wound, the man fell down and cried out, "I am killed"...'

As for Santry, drunk as he was, he mounted his horse and thought he could buy silence by giving four pounds to the landlord. He gave no directions as to what should be done or whether help might be called. This sort of behaviour was something that, had it been committed by any routine highwayman or robber, would have led to a very different outcome.

Laughlin Murphy took a long time to die; he passed away on 25 September, in Hammond Lane in the city. That fact was the saving of Santry. Because death had not been instant, there was an opening for the defence counsel, of course – that it had been disease that had actually caused the death. It only took a skilful lawyer to apply some chop-logic and argue that there was no causation here – that the attack was nothing to do with the death itself. There was no highlighting of such facts that no medical help had been called, no remorse expressed, and so on. The buck had merely thrown a coin and implied that it had better be all hushed up.

Where the turning point lay which led to the acquittal through a reprieve from the King is up for discussion, but certainly a letter written by Dr Thomas Rundle, Archbishop of Perry, mentions one important figure – the Solicitor General, Bowes. Rundle wrote that: 'He did not use one severe word against the unhappy Lord, nor omitted one severe observation that truth could dictate ... But I think he counsel for the prisoner acted detestably. They only prompted him to ask a few treacherous questions ...'

In other words, justice was done, because there had quite clearly been the most terrible and callous behaviour on the part of this notorious buck and scoundrel. As Rundle wrote, still with bitterness in his tone:

> 'When the 23 peers returned to give their opinion, their countenances astonished the whole house, and all knew, from the horror in their eyes, and the paleness of their looks, how they were agitated within before they answered the dread question "Guilty upon my honour" and he was so most certainly, according to the law ...'

But Santry never went to the scaffold. In fact, he was awarded a full pardon. The Duke of Devonshire, the Lord Lieutenant of Ireland, had been largely responsible for petitioning George II. If Santry had gone to meet his death, it would have been a beheading; but he lived to carry on his rakish life. He was also attainted, meaning that he had to forfeit his estate, but that was returned to him after the pardon in 1740. A year after his pardon, Santry travelled to see King George II and thank him face to face; his pardon had come from the Lords triers –the Lords appointed who had found him guilty, but all except one of them signed a letter asking for a pardon. As soon as he had seen the King in Germany, the process of redeeming his estates started.

On his death, the Santry title became extinct.

4

Three Tales of 'Legal' Escapes

Sometimes the minutiae within the law machine create all kinds of loopholes which may open up possibilities of hope for the accused who stands in the dock with every expectation of a death sentence. These three stories relate to such escapes through the tight, closely-defined procedural nature of the trial process. They are tales of sheer chance, odd circumstances and incredible good fortune, ironically favouring the criminal. They provide the kinds of crime stories that make legal professionals wince with embarrassment and those readers who believe in fate smile, with a wry acceptance of twisted, unexpected freedom. In one story, of infanticide, one has to feel a sense of justice and relief, as so many unfortunate young women through the eighteenth and nineteenth centuries were tried and sometimes hanged for killing their child, when in fact what was happening was their terrible experience of post-natal psychosis. The other two tales concern hardened villains who must have thought that the devil was taking care of his own when they walked free.

The first story comes from the records of the Crown Cases Reserved, as explained in the Introduction. In 1800, a man called Benjamin Pooley stood before Sir Alan Chambre at the Old Bailey. His crime was theft while employed by the Post Office. Pooley had taken a letter that had a draft for £200 in it. That meant that there were two counts against him; stealing the letter and then taking the draft. It was a felony on which he stood accused, a serious crime at any time. He was a post sorter and so was in a position of trust.

The draft was from one David Thomson in Maidstone, made out to his London bankers; the paper shown as evidence was unstamped. Chambre was to be a judge involved in much controversy just after this trial, principally after his involvement with the Lancashire Luddites, but he must have always recalled this strange affair. Although Pooley was found guilty, there was a technicality and that needed the consultation of other judges. This related to the original indictment: there was no stamp on the draft, so the question for the lawyers was whether or not this was acceptable as an indictment? The judges sat as the Crown Cases Reserved and many of the top legal brains were at work; the Exchequer Chamber was the scene and for the crown there was the Lord Chief Justice, opposite a Mr Knowles who was later to be the Recorder of London.

After prolonged debate it was decided that the conviction was wrong; the indictment could not be called a 'bill' within the Act on which the offence was stipulated. That might have seemed as though Pooley would walk free, but no, he was then tried on a second charge, that of stealing a letter from the post. This was 1801, and that was a capital offence. He was found guilty and sentenced to hang, by Mr Justice Lawrence. But a report of the time explains why he never stood to receive the noose: '... but the court entertaining doubts whether the second section of the Act [7 Geo.III c.50 s.1] applied to servants of the post office, against whose misconduct the first section of that

Old Bailey Sessions House.

A prison ship or 'hulk'.

Act was intended to guard … the legislature did not conceive that the embezzling a letter by those servants was a larceny, reserved the question for the opinion of the judges.'

On 2 May, 1801, Mr Knapp spoke for Pooley and argued that, as the defendant was employed by the post office when he took the letter, he was exempt from the scope of the Act. Pooley was recommended to the crown for a pardon and walked from the court. Amazingly, on both counts, a technicality not specified or omitted from the text of the statute had made a pardon possible.

The second case, also one which came before the Crown Cases Reserved, was one of infanticide. In the early years of the nineteenth century, there were many such cases, and the usual outcome at that time was a death sentence. The fact is that young women, for all kinds of reasons (poverty, shame, stigma, or mental illness) often took the life of a young child and tried to conceal the birth. One such woman was Jane Fletcher, who was tried and convicted, again before Sir Alan Chambre, at Hereford in 1803.

The sentence of death was given, and there was a crowd of other convicts in court at the time, so Chambre, being distracted by these other characters, omitted the part of the judgement that included the direction to have the woman's body dissected and anatomised. That was a common practice then; giving a felon's body to the medical students meant giving the final punishment to the victim's family, as they had no body to bury.

It was only when Chambre was back in his judge's lodgings that he put this right, and he added the relevant section to the sentence on the calendar of prisoners. This was then taken but he still had to remedy this by speaking in open court. Cautiously, he respited Jane Fletcher's sentence until he could resolve that. Jane had four more days of life so that Chambre could consult with other judges on the matter. The great Lord Ellenborough was involved and in his chambers a group of learned men sat to consider the case; no decision was reached so there was an adjournment. Jane would then have three more months in prison awaiting her fate.

The judges met again on 10 June and they were again divided; these were the most learned and experienced legal minds of that time, and at that meeting in Serjeant's Inn were Ellenborough, Chief Justice, Lord Alvanley, the Chief Baron, and all the puisne judges (High Court judges). The only thing they all agreed on was that the omission could have been put right if Chambre had gone back to court after the adjournment, having the prisoner brought up from the court cell, and passing full judgement.

He had not done that, and the decision was that Jane Fletcher be 'reprieved generally.' She was in fact transported.

The final story concerns a horrendous murder of a child and an escape from the noose that nobody would in the least expect at the time. It is about a murderous beast called William Sheen, and he had a child by a woman called Beadle. That was the root of the legal issue – the name of the child.

In May, 1827, after Sheen had been forced to marry the woman (with a gift of £5 to soften the blow) the man came home and was repeatedly brutal to the baby. This came to a head one day when he was left alone in the house, purposely sending out the mother to buy food, and when she came back there was no Sheen, but the sight that met her eyes was horrible in the extreme; the head of the child was on a table, blood seeping from it, and the decapitated trunk of the body was on the bed. Everyone in the area was aroused and there was a hue and cry, but Sheen had gone.

But matters did not end there; unusually, a police officer played detective and set off on the track of the killer, finding out that Sheen was in Wales, at Llanbadarnfawr in

Radnorshire, where he took him prisoner and brought him to trial. Sheen still had the child's blood on his clothes when arrested. On 27 June that year Sheen stood trial at the Old Bailey. It would have been a fairly common occurrence and people there would surely have considered it a formality that Sheen would hang. He was indicted for the murder of William Beadle, but in that surname lay the core of a defence argument. The barrister objected that the definition or description of the dead child was not 'sufficient'. It was pointed out that the baptism register had these words: 'Charles William, the son of Lydia Beadle.' That statement did not show that Beadle was the formal surname.

As Shakespeare wrote of Hotspur, 'He would cavil on the ninth part of a hair ...' So was the case here. The defence argued that the naming was fatal to the indictment, and Mr Justice Holroyd agreed, giving a not guilty verdict.

But Sheen was still held in custody; the indictment was amended and Sheen stood again at trial on 18 July, before Sir James Burrough and Sir Joseph Littledale. But Burrough said, 'The question in this issue is whether the deceased was as well known by the name of Charles William Beadle as by any of the names in the present indictment ... if the prisoner could have been acquitted on the former indictment, he must be acquitted now ...' He asked the jury to consider whether the child would have been known as Charles William Sheen, and if so, then he directed that the prisoner had to be considered as someone who had 'pleaded his acquittal' in the first place.

The result was that the jury thought the child would have been as well known as Beadle as he would by any other names. The defendant was acquitted. Peter Burke, writing at the end of the century, added that: 'The murderer was discharged after a feeling and solemn admonition from the judge. The after career of Sheen was an awful example of how a man can live with the brand of Cain upon him. Sheen was hooted and scouted by the people whenever he was discovered ...'

The killer, freed on an absurd technicality relating to linguistic terminology, ended his life as an alcoholic, after living as an outcast, unable to find anyone, anywhere, who would give him employment. But of all the acquittals in murder trails in the annals of English criminal law, Rex *v.* Sheen must rank as one of the most amazingly wrong-headed affairs.

5

The Long Riston Mystery 1799

This story is about how a simple cluster of recognisances may open up a tale of sensational high drama – and it involves several local families around a village in East Yorkshire. It is a perfect illustration of how documents from the past may open up into whole areas of fascination in the broader narrative of the age.

To establish first of all exactly what a recognisance is; this is a bond, acknowledged in front of a justice or similar officer, the aim being to 'secure an action by the person named on the document.' In other words, lots of people around the village in question saw cruelty going on before them and they went to see the magistrate. Once they had filled in a recognizance, they were committed to play a part in a prosecution.

Beverley, the Yorkshire market town, was trying to keep up with its grand neighbour, York, in the eighteenth century. It felt that it had a dash of culture and gentry. In fact, throughout the eighteenth century, the planning and architectural developments had been impressive. The rebuilding of the town hall came in 1762, and the courthouse and other municipal buildings were to enhance the appearance of this attractive place of social meetings, hostelries, and visitors on their way to the coast. But beneath this lay the usual dark problems and violence of the Georgian years. In fact, it was the setting for a brutal killing of a defenceless little child.

In the last year of the eighteenth century, when the so-called Age of Reason was flowering, the East Riding Assizes were to witness one of the most repulsive and inhuman cases the annals of murder have ever recorded. It happened at the village of Long Riston, a place described in the nineteenth century as,

> '... standing on the high road from Hull to Bridlington, eleven miles from the former place and nineteen from the latter... There are chapels in the village belonging to the primitive and Wesleyan Methodists erected in 1836. The National School was built by subscription for the accommodation of 100 Children ... It is endowed with about £12 per annum, left by Peter Nevill in 1807.'

Around the turn of the century, then, just as religion and local philanthropy were having an effect, there was one little boy who would not be attending that new national school; he was Thomas Hostler.

At the midsummer assizes for 1799 the true nature of the cruel death of little Thomas was recorded for posterity in the careful and ornate longhand of 'B. Ford.' What happened was that the boy's father, William, together with his wife Jane and his sister-in-law, Elisabeth Beal, who had been maltreating little Thomas, went too far. Neighbours could take it no more; they had witnessed extreme cruelty and this had been happening over a long period. Finally, they acted.

Four people of the village took out a recognizance against the three abusers, and at that time the child was not dead. Christopher Hall, Elisabeth Chadwell, Sarah Wray and Mary Ford stated upon oath that the three defendants had physically abused the little boy, most intensively over a period of several weeks in June of that year. That document meant that each of the accusers was bound to pay thirty pounds to his majesty George III if the action failed. There was going to be little chance of that ever happening. What had been done to the boy was savage beyond belief.

Going so far as to take out a recognizance was a serious commitment. The wording on the paper, under which the person had to sign, was:

'The condition of this recognizance is such, that if the above shall personally appear at the next general quarter sessions of this Peace, to be holden in the said Riding and there testify and give evidence on behalf of our Sovereign Lord the King, then his voice shall be heard by the learned magistrate …'

If not, then the person would have to pay a few shillings in a fine. If an ordinary citizen went so far as to sign that statement, then they were serious about their charge.

This was not a case of what some medical historians write of as 'neonaticide'; this was a toddler, in modern language, and what the evil trio was accused of was expressed in the assize records in this way:

'… with their hands and feet and with whips and staves and sticks they did strike and kick, beat and whip over the head and neck and shoulders, back, belly, sides and posteriors, feet and other parts of the naked body of him the said Thomas Hostler in a cruel and inhuman manner giving him by such strikes, beatings and whippings, large and grievous wounds swellings and bruises on the right side of his head about the temples and several large stripes on his neck.'

These assaults, repeatedly administered over the weeks in question and probably before people took notice, were vicious but also almost systematically done, to affect every part of the child's body as if there was an intention to inflict pain and wounds in a certain manner with predesigned effects.

The records make a special mention of the two women involved – Elisabeth Beal and the mother, Jane: 'Jane his wife and Beal did other wrongs to the said Thomas Hostler then and there, did to the great damage of Thomas Hostler and against the peace of the said Lord … did beat, wound and ill-treat so that of his life it was greatly despaired…'

There was special mention of what Jane did between 2 February and 10 April, noting that she savagely battered the child so that he was near death. The accounts and language used there suggest that there was a sadistic pleasure here, a twisted kind of satisfaction in inflicting harm on the little boy. But their time was up, and the law had tracked them down. The boy does appear to have been dead at the time that the jury came to a decision, but this was not expressed in the record, though we know from a separate second action against the trio that he was dead. At the assizes, the foreman of the jury signed the record, along with the witnesses, Will Iveson, Francis Jackson, Mary Ford, Sarah Wray, Elisabeth Maxwell and Christopher Hobbs.

The document, however, hints at another mystery and at another story, because initially the word 'guilty' was written after the names of all three, but then the word 'guilty' after William Hostler's name was lined through. 'Not guilty' was written after that.

Cobb Hall tower, Lincoln Castle.

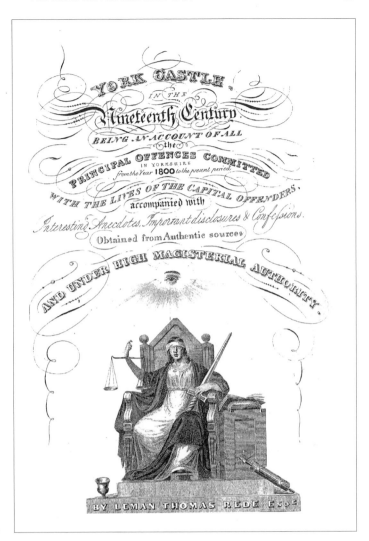

Title page to Rede's
stories of the condemned.

We must assume that the child died just before of the proceedings, though it is not openly stated. However, in a second recognizance, one John Dawson of Beverley swore that he would appear before the next general sessions 'to proffer a bill of indictment against William Hostler, wife and Beal.' On that document the sentence is added: 'For the murder of the infant Thomas.' The date of this document is 1 June, so the child had died just before that.

We have the strange tale of why William Hostler was acquitted, however. Why was the word 'guilty' expunged from the record and why was he released? We have to speculate on reasons for this. Perhaps there was another narrative beyond this one, something relating to family morality or to the fact that at one point the man was trying to take the blame for his wife. But this seems unlikely, given that several people appear to have had a close knowledge of what was going on in the Hostler household. Cynically, we might wonder if he had friends in high places. Whatever the reason, there is a tantalising untold story in the crossing-out of that word, *guilty*. The simple but obvious answer might just be that he was the head of a household and that some local thinking thought that he should remain so that the estate and property (and his work) could keep on. But in the second recognizance he is named, by John Dawson. Two conditions of recognizance named him.

The two women were in for a hard time; they were to be pilloried, then sent to York Castle and from there transported. The pillory had been only recently maintained in Beverley, and this was often combined with whippings, as illustrations from the period make clear. Not until an act of 1837 was the pillory abolished. Stocks and pillories were widespread at the time of this murder, though. There were over eleven thousand pillories in England in 1700.

With a terrible local crime such as this, repugnant to all the sound family values on which the community was based, there was a call for humiliation as well as for the villains to disappear into York, out of sight and mind. Whippings in public were a related punishment, such as the fate of Thomas Roberts of Beverley who was whipped in 1822 for stealing two pairs of women's shoes. It would have seemed a proper administering of natural justice to the locals; the thought that the cruel mother who had applied a whip to her child would now feel the sting of the lash on her back.

Jane and Elisabeth were to spend some time in the dark hovels within York Castle and then be shunted onto a cart, taken to a ship and given the tough experience of a journey to Van Dieman's Land. Statistics at that time would have been against their survival.

Of course, in the words quoted above, stating exactly what the witness had seen and heard going on at the farm where the Hostler's conducted their campaign of cruelty and torture, would be as spoken before an officer of the law. The specific words give the family historian that very rare thing, a sense of how an ancestor would have expressed themselves; a snippet of oral history, in fact. It is not difficult to imagine the emotions in such an action; openly accusing a neighbour and being bound to appear in court to testify, face to face.

As a coda to the story, it is interesting to note that in 1867, one of the most repugnant crimes in Yorkshire in this category also happened at Beverley, when Mary Haldenby thrashed her weak and half-starved son simply for stealing some few bits of food from a neighbour. Again, it was a neighbour, Mary Allen, who had contacted the constable; she almost certainly saved the life of young William; the boy was regularly beaten, by his mother and by the common law husband in the house.

What we have in the Long Riston story is a case of local or regional mores, social habits and conventional behaviour, being too extreme; what was often an established parental action had been extended into a transgression; a line had been crossed from domestic discipline to a criminal offence. In a society in which the grammar schools still taught Latin by the rules of Quintilian, to teach by using the cane and belt, and in which a remonstrance to a child was often accompanied by a slap on the face, it took extreme cruelty to cause a stir. Long Riston felt that revulsion in a wave of disgust in 1799.

6

James Hadfield 1800

On 15 May, 1800, James Hadfield, a man who had served with the Duke of York in the European wars, stopped at a shop belonging to a Mr Harman in Greenhill's Rents, Smithfield, and talked about two pistols he had with him. He said that he had bought them for eight shillings, and he would clean them and sell them for a profit. He then left one of the guns in the shop, saying it might frighten his wife. He must have seemed a definite eccentric to Mr Harman, but he was not the only man who saw Hadfield on this day; in another shop he bought some gunpowder and spoke cryptically about 'a particular business' he had to see to on that day. He drank brandy and went on his way.

The particular business became clear to all present at Drury Lane theatre that night when Hadfield, terribly scarred on the face from his battle experience, stood on a bench, pointed a gun at King George III who had just arrived at the theatre, and fired. George had been responding to the cheers of the crowd, and the bullet missed him by about a foot, lodging in the plaster above him. This happened as the national anthem was being played. Within seconds, courtiers had covered the King and moved into protective positions. Hadfield was grabbed by several people, including two musicians, and dragged away, taken to the music room after being hurled over the rails of the orchestra pit.

James Hadfield saw the Duke of York, the King's son, approach, and said, 'God bless your royal highness, I like you very well, you are a good fellow. This is not the worst that is brewing.' As witnesses spoke at the trial in the hands of Lord Kenyon, it became increasingly clear that Hadfield was deranged. He had received his worst wounds in a fight near Lisle and had been so severely injured that he had been left for dead. It was known in some quarters that he had suffered mental problems since that day. In court, it appeared to the prosecution that he knew exactly what he was doing and had planned an assassination; after all, he had spoken to people en route to the theatre, and he had chosen the best spot in the place from which to fire at the royal box.

The charge was treason, because the man had 'imagined the death of the King' as the Treason Act stated. But Hadfield claimed that he had not planned to kill King George. There had to be testimony from two witnesses that he had planned and attempted the murder, because the offence was treason; but that also enabled him to have two lawyers defend him, and he was fortunate in having Thomas Erskine lead the defence. He was a very talented lawyer, the son of the Earl of Buchan; he had served in the navy, but he changed careers to study law and was admitted to Lincoln's Inn in 1775. He was called to the bar in 1778 and he made his reputation with his defence of Thomas Baillie who had published an attack on Lord Sandwich with regard to abuses in the government of the Greenwich hospital.

But Erskine would have his work cut out with the Hadfield case. Luckily, some of the testimony, such as that by a Mr Wright, made it clear that Hadfield had been 'very confused and agitated' while standing on the bench. People nearby had assumed he was there because he wanted the best view of the King, but the facts seemed to be otherwise. However, it was Hadfield's behaviour in court that began to turn things in his favour. He had sat and stared into space, seeming unconcerned that he was potentially going to be sentenced to be hung, drawn and quartered. But it was the testimony of the Duke of York that turned the matter towards the issue of insanity. The Duke reported what had been said in the music room when the man had been restrained. He said that Hadfield had said he was 'tired of life' and that he 'only regretted the fate of the woman who would shortly be his wife.' What begins to emerge is a picture of a tough soldier who had, in the vocabulary of 2009, suffered 'post traumatic stress disorder' and then other statements made it clear that all was not well in the accused's mind. For instance, Joseph Richardson said that Hadfield had said of the Duke of York, 'God bless him he is the soldier's friend and love!' and had said he had no desire to kill the King.

There had been a frenzy of shooting, though. Other bullets were found, one being in the box occupied by Lady Milner. At that point it must have seemed that, although Hadfield had done and said some very strange things, insanity was not really evident, and there had been rational planning of the act.

But then Erskine spoke. He focused on the question of intention: did Hadfield have a malicious intent to murder the King or was he governed by a 'miserable and melancholy insanity?' Erskine had the full biography of this tragically crazed ex-soldier; he said that Hadfield's real intention had been suicide on that night at the theatre, and that he had conceived the idea that if he fired near the King, he would be arrested and killed, so the suicide would be done in that way. He had thought of firing over the King's coach, for instance.

But then there came the material on the personal life of the accused. Apparently, Erskine said, the man had tried to kill his own daughter just a few days before this attempted killing, and this was done because he thought 'his time had come and he did not want to leave the child behind.' Erskine had a long line of friends and military colleagues who then came to speak, and a full picture emerged of a mind unhinged. One soldier testifying said he had heard Hadfield say that he was King George, calling for a looking glass, and feeling for a crown on his head. Another man said that he had seen the accused 'in a paroxysm of madness' trying to kill him with a bayonet. Other army witnesses stated that Hadfield had been an ideal and excellent solider before the fight at Lisle. This all was said of a man who had once been a royal orderly to the Duke – now a sad discharged soldier with horrible disfigurements and a profoundly disturbed state of mind.

The notion of insanity was therefore before the court. The succession of witness statements on that theme had persuaded Lord Kenyon that this was a man who was mentally insane, and he said that Hadfield could not be found guilty. His destiny was not a date with the axe or the rope, but a journey to Newgate and then Bedlam, from where he would never emerge again into normal life.

The result of the Hadfield case was that, only four days after the trial, a bill was passed with a long title: 'A bill for regulating trials for High Treason and Misprision of High Treason in certain cases, and for the safe custody of Insane Persons charged with Offences.' The main part of this became the Criminal Lunatics Act of 1800. This established the idea of the lunatic being kept at His Majesty's Pleasure, and although it anticipated in some ways the McNaghten Rules as discussed in chapter 2, it was not accurate or learned on the matter of what constituted insanity. But it did require the detention of an insane person, the disposition being done without any work on the part of the judge; it was an automatic destination for men like Hadfield. Before this Act, any person acquitted because of insanity simply walked free unless the judge wanted the person detained; in that case there had to be a civil hearing. The only option open to the court was to use the 1744 Vagrancy Act, which enabled criminals to be detained in a house of correction. But as a defence, a claim of insanity was very difficult to establish. It was a matter of the expertise of the lawyer, and even then, proving insanity before a felony such as murder or treason was very hard. Luckily for Hadfield, he had plenty of people to speak for him, and it was only because the charge was treason, and not murder, that there was full opportunity for a sound defence to be arranged. He had arguably the best legal mind in the land on his side too. Lord Birkenhead, writing in 1910, pointed out the significance of the case: 'This brief, real-life tragedy is unique … it brought a royal Duke into the witness-box and a former royal orderly into the dock.'

7

Hall and Morrison 1817

This is a story that went from horseplay to prison and from prison to a death sentence. It concerns a drunken night in a graveyard and a cause celebre that stirred everyone in Wolverhampton in an effort to save two soldiers from the noose.

It all began in Wolverhampton on 23 July, 1817 when John Hall and Patrick Morrison of the 95th Foot went drinking and stayed out so late that they could not get back into their lodgings. They were also turned away from the guard-room and so wandered into the graveyard. There they met another waif and stray, a bricklayer's labourer from Hertford who was looking for work. He was called John Read, and he was a sporty type, out for some fun, and he and Hall started to wrestle in a friendly way, to pass the time. St Peter's churchyard became the scene of a supposed crime, because in the first fall, Read won, and then in the second, Hall won, and a shilling and a penny dropped from Read's pocket, to be collected by Hall who said, 'It will do for beer!'

What happened then was that the three men wandered around; Read was teased about the money, but then he became aggressive and moaned about the money, so around five in the morning, a watchman saw the three in the market place and was aware of the banter about the wrestling and the cash. Read changed his attitude and openly said that he would have them charged with theft or even robbery. Then a local grocer became aware of the situation and it was his chat with the keeper of the local house of correction, George Roberts, who was interested and said, 'This will be a job for us.' Roberts questioned Read about the night's events and then went on to arrest the two soldiers. The charge was that they had robbed Read 'on the highway' – and that meant it would be a capital offence. Although Read said that he had been knocked down and robbed in the church yard, nevertheless, the commitment of the soldiers to Stafford assizes was for highway robbery. They were to stand trial for their lives.

It was felt by all concerned that Read would naturally say that there had been a fight which would be interpreted in legal terms as a 'common assault.' With that in mind, it was assumed that the matter would end with perhaps a fine, and that the court would be aware that drink was involved, and that Read himself was compliant with the fooling around in the churchyard, as that evening had been a typical night out with men drinking and sporting around for fun.

That was until the terrible news broke. *The Times* reported this very dramatically:

'An old man was reading the paper in an ale-house to a number of politicians, who were not much affected at anything they heard, until he came to that part which stated which persons left for execution. Amongst the names were those of Hall and Morrison. The whole population of Wolverhampton instantly showed how they felt upon an occasion so dreadful.'

There was a meeting of local people, and the Rev. Guard, who had known Hall since he was a child, came to play a part. He was convinced that Hall was incapable of such a robbery and was sure that there had been a terrible mistake. He actually tracked the judge, Baron Garrow, on his assize circuit to talk to him. Sir William Garrow was known as a 'hanging judge' and so that was to be a tall order. But he faced him and took issue with the decision, saying, 'I see you are determined to hang these poor men!' Garrow was offended and the result was that he would not flinch. Guard, however, sure that he had to carry on and try another gambit, went right to the top and arranged to see Lord Sidmouth, the Home Secretary. They spoke for four hours and Sidmouth was known to comment that he had never known such importunities from someone who was not a blood-relative of the condemned. There was some cause for optimism on Guard's part when he left, but even so, the opinion of the judge in any assize case was paramount.

But Guard was not the only one in Wolverhampton who was deeply concerned at this injustice. There had been another meeting, and prominent in that was the part played by Mr Charles Mander, of the varnish manufacturing company in the area. Mander and the other prominent people of the town put together a petition to the Prince Regent on the matter. A Mr Pearsall, a silk-mercer from Cheapside, was asked to recount the events in the churchyard, and there were affidavits created for Sidmouth, and just as the Secretary was dealing with the Recorder's Reports, he noted all this activity and put the statements in the hands of the Attorney General. At that point there was some hope.

Sidmouth was the party involved in the case who swung things in the soldier's favour, saying that the material gathered by Mander and Pearsall made him feel assured that the two men should not be hanged, and he posted a respite to the sheriff. He is on record as saying that he could not endure 'one hour more of unnecessary anxiety.'

There was then an investigation, and the focus was on Roberts of the house of correction; it became clear that Roberts had been greedy for what was called 'blood money' – he would earn £80 for the arrest. Roberts had realised that he could make the odd events of that night fit another narrative, one that would allow him to arrest them and take cash under what was called the 'Parliamentary Rewards System.' This meant that a person who made an arrest for a felony and then the court process led to a hanging could claim the 'blood money.' Obviously, this was a desperate attempt, passed as a statute under William and Mary in 1701 as a measure to bring in ordinary people as thief-takers – in a society without a police force, of course. Roberts had gone to Read, heard the account of the night and then concocted a story that would fit the offence of highway robbery. He had then gone with other men to arrest the soldiers at the Fox Inn and they were then taken to a clerical magistrate at Tettenhall.

The trial at Stafford before Garrow had been a travesty: there were no witnesses and no-one had been there to speak on the soldiers' behalf; but all had turned out well thanks to the efforts of several men, notably Guard and Mander. Charles Mander actually made a copy of Sidmouth's respite, and he came home with that, triumphant. This is the text of the respite:

HOME OFFICE

Enquiry into the confession made by David John Ware of the murder of Olive Balchin in respect of which murder Walter Graham Rowland was convicted at Manchester Assizes on the 16th December, 1946

Report by
MR. JOHN CATTERALL JOLLY, K.C.

*Presented by the Secretary of State for the Home Department
to Parliament by Command of His Majesty
February, 1947*

Left: Stafford Courthouse.

Below: Convicts on their way to transportation.

Whitehall

13 August, 1817

Sir,

I am to signify to you his Royal Highness the Prince Regent's commands in the Name
And on the behalf of His Majesty, that the execution of the Sentence of Death passed
upon
John Hall and Patrick Morrison, now in gaol at Stafford, should be respited until the
further signification of His Royal Highness's Pleasure.

I am Sir

Your most obedient servant

Sidmouth.

That was sent to the High Sheriff of the County of Stafford. A crowd of 2,000 people
were waiting to meet Mander with the copy of this reprieve; he stepped out of the mail
coach and read out the reprieve. It took a month for the free pardon to be issued, and
of course, the respite was simply the first stage, merely putting off the hanging; the
two men were not released until 17 September, when they were invited to dine at the
Mander's house, taking their wives with them. Their story ended happily, as the press
reported: 'The Home Office stated, that Baron Garrow, upon reading the affidavits, said
if the facts had been known before, their respite should have been granted, and asked
whether they would, upon being pardoned, be taken into the regiment again. Lieutenant
Buchanan immediately replied that they would be most gladly received.'

As for George Roberts, who had lusted for the blood money, his house of correction
did not last long, although he survived the enquiry into his conduct. An inspection of
Wolverhampton house of correction in 1820 led to the closure of the awful place, a foul
and neglected hell which the inspector, William Dyott, had found to be in a 'most filthy,
dirty, shameful state.'

The Act, which created the notion of 'blood money', was repealed in June, 1818, after
some good work by Charles Mander and the great reformer Samuel Romilly. A petition
from Stafford had played a major part in changing attitudes to that fearful statute,
something that would always be a temptation to men like Roberts, who could bend the
facts of a story to their evil advantage.

8

Not Proven: Madeleine Smith 1857

There is something about this suspected case of poisoning that has captured the imagination of the classic true crime writers. F. Tennyson Jesse and William Roughead have written at length about the story of the sweet little middle class Glasgow girl who had a romantic attachment which would have been forbidden had it been known by her parents. There have been essays and revisionary works looking again at the case, with the writers trying desperately to resolve the question of her guilt.

Madeleine was the daughter of a successful architect in Glasgow, James Smith; the family lived in the city at No. 7 Blytheswood Square except in the summer, when they moved to Row near Gareloch on the coast. The girl was educated in the traditional way for her class and her social position, going to boarding school at Clapton, and showing an aptitude in art and music. But what would have been a merely conventional progress into womanhood, courtship and probable marriage was rocked into emotional intensity when the nineteen-year-old Madeleine was introduced to Pierre L'Angelier. As previous writers have pointed out, even the man's name suggests a certain degree of romance and fantasy, and the sources show that the young man had been worshipping Madeleine from afar for some time before his friend effected an introduction. L'Angelier was born in Jersey, and in 1855 when he met Madeleine, he was working as a clerk. It is apparent that the man saw a profitable marriage as the best and most pleasant route to social success, and he selected Madeleine as the likely candidate for his affections. He had started out on that track of trying to bag a rich young lady already when he professed his undying love for the architect's daughter, having been twice engaged.

As so often happens when there is a relationship very much against the prevailing attitudes to status and the desire to marry an equal, the first stage of the affair was mainly in writing; a long succession of love letters began. Naturally, her father did not approve and the secret could not remain so for long. He found out and someone told him that Madeleine had been spotted out walking with an unknown man; that would have seemed like a potential scandal of the worst kind to a Victorian paterfamilias. In June, 1855, both parents made it clear to their wandering daughter that the match was unacceptable; the French suitor was told in no uncertain terms that he was not welcome. But matters were more serious than it must have appeared to the parents, because L'Angelier's letters insisted that Madeleine had promised to marry him, and so his attitude to her turned cold. He was putting on a performance of the rebuffed lover; he accused her of being devious, saying one thing to her and something else (or nothing) to her father.

But all was definitely not finished between the young lovers, as a fiend reconciled them and their affair continued underground, with them having to move shiftily and guiltily in the shadows as it were. What then developed was a series of nocturnal visits by the young man to the Smith house; this really was unacceptable at that time

– L'Angelier had the help of a servant, Christina Haggart, who opened the door to the young man at night and made sure that they had time together. By the end of the year 1855, their passion was at its height.

They even planned to elope at one point, as the months passed and the illicit assignations became the scenes of more intensity and expressions of devotion. L'Angelier would tap on the window with his stick and then his admittance would be sorted out by Haggart. The letters were passionate to say the least. Madeleine wrote such words as 'Much love, kisses, tender long embraces, kisses … I am they ever fond, thy own dear loving wife, thy MIMI.'

Blytheswood Square, the scene of this passion, became infamous in later years after the trial; the couple worked out a plan of how and when L'Angelier could deliver letters to her, and this entailed the subterfuge of the man walking along outside, stopping as if to tie a shoelace, and then dropping in a letter through a window for Madeleine to collect. One of the best times for a lovers' meeting was a Sunday morning when the parents were at worship in church. All this seems traditional stuff for the affair of the heart against social hierarchy, and the element of wild romance appears to be strong, but in fact, as he was at bottom a fortune-hunter, the young woman could not trust in him; if it had to be kept a secret liaison, something very different from a courtship prior to marriage, then she had to trust him. She trusted an adventurer, and matters began to turn darker when the idea of marriage appeared on the scene.

Madeleine accepted an offer of marriage by a Glasgow businessman called William Minnoch and the first moves towards their friendship reached L'Angelier; he must have been ready with reprisals after she wrote to tell him that she had accepted Minnoch's proposal in January, 1857. L'Angelier threatened to show all her letters to her father. When we consider the potential consequences of such scandal and ruination in the mid-Victorian years, then we can understand Madeleine's response. She wrote, 'It will kill my mother … Oh, will you not keep a secret from the world? Oh you will not, for Christ's sake denounce me! I shall be ruined … Despise me, hate me, but shake me not with a public scandal. Emile, will you not grant me this last favour?' All this pleading had no effect on the man. Some of the letters were given to Mr Smith.

It was blackmail, plain and simple. But the results were far from simple. After a week away at the Bridge of Allan, L'Angelier followed and we assume that they had secret meetings; the Smiths returned and it became apparent that L'Angelier was ill. Madeleine advised him, and her suggestions of improving his health are in print, so that was either a genuine move on her part, or a subtle gambit known to be later in her favour after a crime was done. But on 22 March, there was a marked development in the tale of the lovers; L'Angelier had been feeling very poorly for a few days, and then in the early afternoon of the 22 March he rang the doorbell at his lodgings and his landlady came to the door. L'Angelier was desperately ill on the doorstep and he said, 'I am going to have another attack of the vomiting … I am very bad.'

The man was attended by a Dr Steven, and morphia was prescribed; the patient is on record as having said, 'I know better, I am far worse than the doctor thinks.' He died in his sleep a few hours after the doctor's visit. There were notions that this was a suspicious death and the key person in the emerging events was a man called De Mean. He knew that there had been this illicit affair and he knew that Smith had the dead man's letters. De Mean worked with L'Angelier's employers to pursue matters relating to Madeleine and this awful death. Madeleine foresaw all kinds of nasty developments and in a panic she ran off, taking a boat to Row, where the summer home of her family was.

Minnoch brought her back and from that point the Madeleine Smith story transmutes from a tale of love to a high-profile and scandalous story of a possible murder. In Scotland it is the task of the Procurator Fiscal to handle coroner's affairs in this kind of context and he ordered the body to be exhumed. In the decades before the Arsenic Act of 1851, when there had been an attempt to regulate the dispensation of the poison, the public were aware of the frequency of the use of the poison in murder cases, as the press reported these tales in depth and with relish. Madeleine was charged and arrested. She insisted on her innocence from the start, and pointed out that there had been no clandestine meetings in a period of three weeks before the man's death, so that should exonerate her. But matters were much more complex than that; the fact was that it was known that she had bought arsenic, and her reply was that it was for her complexion really, but that when buying it she had said it was for rats. We have to say that it would have been a little shaming for a woman to admit to using arsenic to whiten the skin (as had been the habit of many wealthy ladies for centuries) but it cannot be denied that the suspicious death and the purchase of poison raised the obvious questions.

The trial in Edinburgh began on 30 June, 1857, at the High Court of Judiciary, and the prosecution had a great deal in their armoury. They had ascertained that the accused had bought arsenic on three occasions, and that the dates of his attacks of pain and vomiting coincided with the purchases. On one occasion, Madeleine had passed some cocoa for him through the bedroom window and Blytheswood House. There was a clear motive, of course; she was being blackmailed and had much to lose if the full story of her liaison with the Frenchman was public knowledge. Prosecution could also prove that they met shortly before the final illness when he staggered on the lodgings doorstep. It was looking black for Madeleine.

The defence response was obvious; the poison was bought for quite legitimate and common purposes, they denied that the deceased had met the accused early on the day of the death, and they disputed the whole business of poison being administered by Madeleine at any time, including the obvious assertion that there was no proof that the cocoa was poisoned. One of the most convincing defence statements concerned the motive; the killing of L'Angelier would have made it totally certain that the incriminating letters would have fallen into the wrong hands, so why would she risk that?

In the course of the trial the possibility of suicide was discussed. This was because there was a notably heavy dose of arsenic in the corpse when examined; that was a possibility. But the key argument was the establishment of an occasion when Madeleine could have administered the fatal dose. There were alibis; her sister had sworn that Madeleine was in bed from ten on the Sunday evening to eight the next day and Haggart backed that up. The defence counsel, Inglis, a man who has been called by one historian 'the brightest ornament of the Scots bar', gave a brilliant and impassioned speech, focusing on the idea of motive with regard to gain (either financial or otherwise) and he used some clever casuistry in his rhetoric, linking the most ridiculous species of 'gain' as potential motive for murder. Along with this argument was an attack on the dead man, making it clear that he had the basest motives for the dishonest and corrupting emotional assault on an innocent young girl.

L'Angelier actually said, according to one witness, 'If she were to poison me I would forgive her.' He had also told the same witness that there were two occasions on which Madeleine had given the man coffee and cocoa, after which he felt very ill. But Inglis turned this around and built it into the character assassination of the dead man. But certainly Madeleine went shopping for poison; on one occasion she had gone out to procure prussic acid, saying to an employee of a chemist that she wanted it for her hands. On the one hand we have the possibility of Madeleine being a wealthy young woman who read the usual ladies' magazines and knew of the latest advice on cosmetics and dress, and did her best to follow up the new ideas, yet on the other hand we have the possibility that she was a cold, calculating killer.

She was not found 'Not guilty' but as this was in Scotland, there was the verdict of 'Not proven.' Lord Hope summed up at length, and seemed to see much sense in the prosecution's thinking on the question of possible motive; but he stressed that there were no witnesses who had seen the lovers together at the crucially important times in the narrative of the death, and that nothing placed L'Angelier at Blytheswood Square within the time-frame required for the process of poisoning symptoms from the outset to the moment of death. It was a majority verdict that returned 'not proven.' If the death had been suicide, then a motive for that is hard to find.

There was some sympathy for the dead young man. After the trial there was a public subscription for L'Angelier's mother at home in Jersey; that raised almost £90, but in contrast, such was the feeling in support of Madeleine in her home town that the sum raised to help her was £5,000. The Courier reported on what Madeleine did after walking from the court: 'Miss Smith, on getting out at Stepps Station … immediately drove to Rowaleyn House, where she arrived a little after ten o'clock. We regret to learn that Mrs Smith (her mother) is in a very critical condition and is rapidly sinking under the calamity which has been brought upon the family by the unfortunate daughter.'

In a letter written just after the verdict, she wrote: 'I was not at all pleased with the verdict but I was charmed with the loud cheer the court gave me. I got out of Edinburgh in the most private manner possible …' A reporter at the time noted the exit from the court, and his words resonate with the deep irony of her 'exit' which was to be in fact only the beginning of her prominence in the annals of serious crime: 'The gate of the dock is thrown open, the trap-door is lifted, and for the last time Madeleine Smith, with her wonted elegant composure, slowly descends the stair, followed to the end by the eager gaze of the multitude, and so passes from the ken of her contemporaries.'

Madeleine Smith died in America in April, 1926, at the age of 92. She had earlier emigrated to Australia and then on to America, married several times, and was a subject of interest on and off for the media throughout her long life. She may have escaped the noose, but she never escaped notoriety. Undoubtedly her social class and status were a factor in her escape; only twelve years before her trial, Eliza Joyce had been hanged for poisoning her husband, and in 1868, Priscilla Biggadike, since proved innocent, was hanged at Lincoln for the same crime. In the broader Victorian picture, we can see the link between females and murder by poison as the focus of how the culture saw 'the fairer sex' – should they kill, then the condemnation, and the punishment, was severe indeed.

But in the case of Madeleine Smith, the wonderful edge of uncertainty survives just as the thinking at the time wavered between guilt and innocence as rhetoric and legal expertise worked to save her neck.

9

Victoria Under Attack

In March, 1882, Queen Victoria had gone into London to hold a 'Drawing room' social event at Buckingham Palace. After that she and Princess Beatrice went back to Windsor on the Thursday afternoon (March 2nd) by train from Paddington. Arriving at Windsor at almost five-thirty, Victoria crossed the platform to walk to her waiting carriage. She and Beatrice stepped inside and as the outrider moved, so did the carriage, but at that moment, as cheers were raised all around, a young man walked out with a gun in his hand and fired at the carriage.

He was Roderick Maclean and luckily he was a poor shot. The driver moved off smartly and the gunman was overhauled, grabbed by the intrepid Superintendent Hayes of Windsor police. With him was Inspector Fraser of the Metropolitan Police, an officer assigned to the Royal Household. Shabby Maclean from Victoria Cottages in Windsor was set about by the public as well, including two Eton scholars who attacked him with an umbrella. When the young man was securely held, he said, 'Don't hurt me, I did it through starvation …' He had fired two ball cartridges from his German pistol. The bullet meant for the Queen missed the carriage and hit a truck beyond.

Maclean went to trial in Reading and was declared insane. He was a pathetic figure, having just a few coppers on his person when searched, and it was reported that he lived 'an idle life in beggarly poverty.' He was later given a state trial and he was found guilty of what was, of course, a capital offence. He was found not guilty on the grounds of insanity. The charge was 'traitorously and maliciously compassing the death of her Majesty the Queen and with having on March 2 discharged a pistol loaded with powder and bullet at Her Majesty.' One report at the time said: 'The prisoner took his place calmly … During the time he had been in prison his clothes had got shabbier than when he was arrested …'

Maclean was, of course, in an asylum for the course of his natural life. *The Penny Illustrated Paper* reported on the closing moments of the trial:

> 'On being called upon to plead, the prisoner said, "Not guilty my Lord". The case was then outlined by the Attorney General, who called the witnesses … Mr Montague Williams called witnesses who gave clear proofs of Maclean's insanity. The jury retired at twenty minutes to five and after five minutes' deliberation, returned into court and delivered a verdict of Not Guilty on the grounds of insanity. The Lord Chief Justice ordered the prisoner to be detained under Her Majesty's Pleasure.'

Queen Victoria and various members of her family tended to travel without much fear of attack. Often they rode in an open carriage and only one or two staff members of the Royal Household would be around. Illustrations in contemporary books and periodicals show the open-topped carriages of royalty, often without much awareness of security.

The picture from *The Illustrated London News* showing Maclean's attack makes it clear that there was a horseman in front of the carriage, but no escort to the side who might have blocked the would-be assassin's view and his shot, of course. Partly this was because of the certainty that Victoria, centre of the vast British Empire, was adored by all. Men and women were giving their lives across the world for that ideal, serving her wherever the map was painted red.

But she was also a target and of the nature of what would now be called a 'celebrity target.' Not only had there been an intruder into her rooms at Buckingham Palace, but in the year of her wedding to Prince Albert, 1840, there had been a much more threatening attack. This was by a teenage pot boy who was out of work. He was in a secret society, some said, and may well have been a stooge in a wider plot. It was a time of active radical violence and there were some factions in society who wanted the Queen dead.

Edward Oxford took advantage of the couple taking an evening ride in an open carriage along Constitution Hill; the young man, who had been standing in Green Park,

ATTEMPT
To Assassinate
THE QUEEN
And PRINCE ALBERT.

Yesterday evening as her Majesty & Prince Albert were taking their evening ride in an open carriage, about six o'clock, & when they had proceeded a little way up Constitution Hill, a man who was standing on the side next to the Green Park, took a pistol from his breast & fired it at her Majesty. The Prince, who probably observed the action of the man, placed his hand behind her Majesty's head & pressed it forward, to which, under Providence, her preservation may be owing. The man immediately fired another pistol, but happily with as little effect. The Prince directed the carriage to proceed as if nothing had happened. The villain who made this diabolical attempt was seized by a number of persons who rushed towards him, & on the arrival of the police he was taken to Queen Square Office. Her Majesty rose in the carriage immediately after the discharge of the first pistol, and as the second was fired as rapidly as if it had been the second shot in a duel. The reports of both pistols were very loud.

The indignation expressed by the surrounding gentry, and, indeed, all parties who had heard of the nefarious attempt, was most unequivocally expressed. There was an immense number of horsemen and carriages drawn up in the Park, extending from the statute of Achilles to the Park, and her Majesty as she approached, the most lively and loyal cheering was manifested, and the air was literally rent with enthusiastic shouts and greetings.

FURTHER PARTICULARS.

On being taken to the station-house, he gave his name EDWARD OXFORD, a native of Birmingham, 17 years of age, and lived as pot-boy at the Hog-in-the-Pound, Mary-le-Bone Lane, facing Oxford Street, and that he had a room at No. 6, West Street, West Square, on searching of which the police found a sword and a black crape cap made to fit the face, a powder flask and bullets which fitted the pistols.

The prisoner will be examined this day at the Home Office.
BIRT, Printer, 39, Great St, Andrew Street, Seven Dials.

A poster on the attempted killing of Victoria.

A picture showing how vulnerable the royals were in transit.

came forward with a gun in his hand and fired it at Her Majesty. Prince Albert saved the Queen's life, as he put his hand behind her head and pushed it forward. He had seen the assassin come to them and saw what was going to happen.

A pamphlet at the time reported that the young man was soon captured, but not before he fired a second shot from another pistol, which missed the target. The report says: 'The prince directed the carriage to proceed as if nothing had happened. The villain who made this diabolical attempt was seized by a number of persons who rushed towards him, and on the arrival of the police he was taken to Queen's Square office.'

Oxford was from Birmingham and he had been working as a pot boy at a tavern called The Hog in the Pound on the Marylebone Road. When his room in West Street was searched there were some sinister revelations; they found a black crepe cap and powder flask, along with pistols. One report on the incident said, 'the true moral courage of our beloved sovereign had ruled supreme.'

In 1842, John Francis tried to take the Queen's life and this time two bullets were fired at her. He was convicted of using gunpowder and other destructive material and sentenced to death. But Francis had his sentence commuted to life imprisonment. Amazingly, she was still moving around in a brash and fearless way when, just two days after Francis' attempt, a man called John William Bean fired a loaded pistol at her. Again she survived, and public opinion was a mix of deep concern and astonishment that nothing more active was being done to protect her. Bean was called a 'hunchback miscreant' by *The Illustrated London News* reporter. The police reacted to this by rounding up all the deformed young men they could come across, in a stupid reaction. But Bean had escaped from custody and he had escaped; the two constables in charge of him were sacked. Yet the Queen's brazen facing of danger and refusal to break routine could only increase the love and respect her people had for her. She went to the opera shortly after the 1842 attacks, and as she entered her box there was a loud applause and the performance had to stop as there was a 'demonstration of the liveliest joy' from the crowd.

In 1872, just after the Prince of Wales had recovered from an illness which almost took his life, again she was returning from a drive in the park when another young man, this time a politically motivated assailant called Arthur O'Connor, pointed a pistol at her as she was about to leave her carriage. A biographer got the facts wrong on this one, reporting that 'Two days after the Thanksgiving, a lad named O'Connor made an attempt to kill the Queen ... the lad was seized by John Brown, the favourite attendant of our sovereign.' It was not an attempt to kill as the gun was not loaded, and later, police found on the young man a knife and a parchment on which was framed a petition for the release of the Fenian prisoners. He said he was ready to die and asked to be shot, not hanged. In effect, he was given twenty years' hard labour and twenty strokes with the birch. Victoria had screamed and hurled herself across Lady Churchill, to see John Brown in charge of the situation as she recovered her composure. O'Connor was simply acting alone – he was not part of any major Fenian plot.

O'Connor was a scholarly type, but he had been working in a paint factory for some time after dallying in political ideas for a while; his mother later said that the boy had experienced what we would now call a mental breakdown, but she noted that he had destroyed his writings and began to wander the streets aimlessly. It became known that the boy's real intention was simply to stand and accost the Queen but had been frightened at the police presence. At the trial, there was the strange event of both John Brown and Prince Leopold, who had been in the carriage, appearing in court, and the Scotsman drew the lion's share of attention, of course, saying that he had seen the young gunman and 'gied him a bit shove back ... I took hold o' him with one of ma hands and I grippit him with the other by the scruff o' the neck ...' Leopold tried to tell the court that the real hero of the day had been his brother Arthur, and Victoria did not like that one bit.

Oddly, a doctor considered O'Connor fit to plead in court at the Old Bailey; his insanity was assumed, but the sentence was thought by many to be very light – one year of hard labour and a flogging. But the reasons why he made the attack were not to be made public and, in spite of the Queen's attempt to have the man's sentence extended to seven years, matters remained unchanged.

But none of this really changed the Queen's habits. What it did do was affect the work of the police, of course. The attacks made the authorities far more aware of the potential disasters of assassination, as the death of a major figurehead, a symbol of massive wealth and power, would have all kinds of repercussions across the globe. Scotland Yard has steadily formed a more sophisticated tranche of provisions for royal protection, so that we now have the SO14, which amalgamated with the Royal Palaces Division, to form an important section of the Royal and Diplomatic Protection Department.

These men are the inheritors of the Victorian forces largely drawn from a Division of the Metropolitan Police and the use of the Royal Protection Patrols. But in the attempts on Victoria's life, the horrors of assassination were prevented by a combination of good fortune and prompt action by Prince Albert.

10

Under Seal of the Queen:
Dr Smethurst 1859

This story could almost be called 'the perfect crime.' It is fascinating, and concerns two medical doctors – one a villain and one a celebrated pathologist in his time. Even more unusual, we have a detailed memoir from the barrister who conducted the prosecution. To this day, the guilt of Dr Thomas Smethurst has not been established.

It all began when Isabella Banks, a wealthy woman who chose not to live at home with her family, but took lodgings instead, found herself staying at a place in Bayswater. Isabella had a personal fortune of £2,000 – a very large sum indeed in 1859 – and in the lodgings there was also a married couple, Smethurst and his wife. The doctor was twenty years younger than his wife; he was fifty years old at the time, and he was attracted to Isabella, who responded to his advances. They became very close, and naturally the landlady noticed this. She asked Isabella to leave the place and only a few weeks later, Smethurst followed her.

Early in 1859, Isabella and Smethurst were married at Battersea Church. Although this was bigamous, the first wife did not act. The barrister writing about the case in 1882, noted that, 'Oddly enough, no surprise was expressed by the doctor's wife, and her position in the affair is very difficult to be understood.' The new married couple moved to a new address in the London suburbs and from that point, as was known afterwards, Isabella began to be ill. As she was rich, she was seen by a celebrated doctor with a good reputation called Julius, and he confirmed that she was not pregnant, but that there was a problem with her digestion. He was worried, and called in some more advice; the sick woman's sister came, and poor Isabella's condition deteriorated. A second medical expert was called for and he said directly: 'That lady is being poisoned.'

Arsenic was found in Isabella's vomit, and by this time there were three doctors involved, the last being Dr Taylor who was very well known at that time. Together, they agreed that the law must be contacted and they asked for a warrant for Smethurst's arrest. Amazingly, at the magistrate's court, Smethurst spoke about the possible fatal effects of his being away from his wife when she was in such desperate circumstances. There was apparently a disastrous level of naivety and amateurism at that court and he was released. But Isabella Banks (she was not Mrs Smethurst by law) died a few days later, on 3 May. There was a post mortem examination, and not only was arsenic found in her body, but also antimony. The latter would be in the form of tartar emetic. If a large dose had been administered by Smethurst, along with the arsenic, then poor Isabella would have had a terrible and agonising period of dying, as antimony causes severe burning in the throat and constant vomiting and diarrhoea; her limbs would have taken on a bluish tinge.

The landlady in the lodging house where the poor woman was dying stated that Smethurst was the only person taking care of the patient, as he would not pay a nurse, and she told the press that 'no portions of the food sent up to the room ever returned.'

What Smethurst did next is repulsive in the extreme and points the finger of guilt at the man. The barrister, Ballantyne, tells the story:

> 'On Saturday, the 12th April, preceding the death, the accused man went to a solicitor and requested him to call at his lodgings the next day for the purpose of drawing out a will, at the same time showing him a draft that a barrister had prepared. The solicitor objected to doing so on a Sunday but being told that the lady was ill, consented ... The lawyer wished that a medical man could be present but that was denied ... a will was drawn up which left everything to the accused ...'

Smethurst was arrested. The trial was before Lord Chief Baron Pollock, but before we recall the nature of the court events, we must return to the forensics, such as they were, at the time. The Dr Taylor who was the last medical man to be called in to see the patient was famous and admired for his post mortem work, but the barrister Ballantyne was convinced that Smethurst had set up the celebrated doctor to fail. After Smethurst was released from the magistrate's court, he found a way to get into his own rooms, and set a trap that would cancel out Taylor's attempts to prove the act of arsenic poisoning; he left a bottle of colourless liquid along with other materials and instruments that a medical man would have. When Taylor later examined all this, his attention was drawn to the liquid, of course; the test he would have used was called the Reinsch test, the standard test for detecting the presence of arsenic.

At the post mortem there was the undoubted fact that there was arsenic present in the body, but Taylor had to show that it had been given from the equipment in Smethurst's room. The test involved pouring a mixture of the tested liquid and hydrochloric acid onto some copper gauze, which would then attach itself to the liquid if there was arsenic present. But the gauze dissolved. Finally, after several attempts, some attachment was done and so the doctor told the court that there was arsenic detected in Smethurst's liquid, but then scientists for the defence reported on the bottle and its contents and stated with confidence that it was chlorate of potash. It was then shown that the only arsenic Taylor had found was in his own gauze – traces being there from the first two experiments.

The result was that there was no credence given to the scientific evidence of the prosecution. In 1859, arsenic was being used by women for cosmetic purposes, as discussed in chapter 8, and of course, there could have been antimony from tartar emetic used as a treatment – an effort to make the poor woman vomit out the arsenic.

The barrister Ballantyne was so confident that Smethurst had done all this to fool Taylor that he consulted a doctor who had found a letter from Smethurst in a copy of *The Lancet* a few years earlier, and this was good detective work, because on the next page to that letter there was a feature article by a famous chemist, explaining how, if chlorates were used, the Reinsch test would be rendered useless. Ballantyne adds in his memoirs, '... I have never been able to make up my mind whether there was really any poison in the bottle, or whether it was a contrivance which had been arranged for the purpose during the interval between the prisoner's first and second apprehensions ... but whatever the intention, it undoubtedly saved his life.'

What Ballantyne did point out was that Dr Taylor, after the event, tried to gather expert advice on the matter, but in the end, the barrister's thoughts are hard to argue with; he said, 'The difficulty that presents itself to my thoughts is, why the presence of the chlorate was not ascertained before the test was applied.'

At the Old Bailey, in August 1859, the sentence of death was passed on Thomas Smethurst. Then there began several months of appeals for a reprieve. The Lord Chief Baron passed the death warrant and it was arranged that Smethurst be taken from Newgate to the county gaol of Surrey, Horsemonger Lane. The doctor was incessantly talking of his innocence and he was obsessed with Dr Taylor, who he claimed was so concerned with his good reputation that he would see a man die rather than admit shortcomings.

At that time, executions took place two weeks after sentence and once again, incident and drama were part of this extraordinary man's life. *The Times* reported on 22 August that: 'Some doubts appear to be entertained, notwithstanding the conviction of the prisoner, whether the capital sentence will be carried out.' This was based on a report about opinions 'from a high quarter.' The Chief Baron, passing sentence, had left out the statements about the prisoner preparing to leave this world. It was said that 'persons well qualified to form a judgement' on the matter thought that there would be a recommendation for clemency. But a week later nothing in that respect had happened. There was still a rumour that the Home Secretary had sent a respite to Smethurst, but all the press could do was keep the public's appetite for news of the prisoner on the boil by documenting the situation.

The condemned man was said to have a calm and indifferent demeanour and, even when his usual clothes were removed and he was given prison issue clothes, there was still mystery and intrigue surrounding him, such as the speculation that it was thought he might have some poison hidden in garments that he might use to forestall the hangman. When the Rev. Jessop went to see Smethurst to confirm the execution date and to advise him spiritually, the reported response was that if he were to become a waxwork at Madame Tussaud's in his prison dress he would look 'a complete guy.' And he added: 'If the sentence is carried out, I am a murdered man.'

The doctor's argument to anyone who would listen is that such were the dimensions of the investments made by Isabella Banks that she would have been the source of greater profits for him if alive rather than dead. He also said that his nursing of the woman in her last days, excluding all others, was done from care, not control of a slow killing. Then by 2 September, the clamouring for a respite by various parties, represented by Henry Sheridan, resulted in a meeting with the Home Secretary in which a petition was presented. The doctor's wife and the landlady from Bayswater were also present, and Sir George Lewis listened to statements and arguments and talked of the prisoner for an hour and a half. Nothing was resolved, and the date with the hangman was very near.

Then, three days later, the announcement was in the press:

'The greatest anxiety appears to exist in the public mind as to the ultimate fate of Dr Smethurst. But of course, no determination has yet come upon the subject ... all that is at present known is that the execution of the capital sentence having been respited during Her Majesty's Pleasure, the life of the culprit will undoubtedly be spared ...'

He had the reprieve, but he did not know the nature of the commutation of sentence or of any other fate. The supporters of the saved man were still working hard to have a total remission of the sentence given.

But as he was awaiting trial for bigamy, the end of the murder trial and the complex consequences came in the form of a free pardon from Queen Victoria. In Southwark magistrate's court, a free pardon was read aloud by a Mr Robinson, with the powerful and redeeming words at the head: 'Under the Seal of Our Lady the Queen.' The pardon stated: 'We, in consideration of some circumstances humbly represented to us, are graciously pleased to extend our grace and mercy unto him, the said Thomas Smethurst, and to grant him a free pardon ...'

Yet even that is not the end of the story. In December that year, a correspondent to *The Times* pointed out that as Smethurst, who after the pardon had been given a year's prison sentence for bigamy at the Old Bailey, was a felon, he would forfeit his inheritance. As the writer expressed it: 'The effect of his conviction ... precludes him from obtaining a single farthing under the will.' He went on to point out that the City of London 'under ancient jurisdiction' had the right to claim property of felons in its domain. Smethurst in court was found guilty because the jury presumed his first marriage to be a valid one after Smethurst's counsel had been unable to convince the court of the invalidity of the union with 'Mrs Johnson' as she was sometimes known.

The final irony has to be that Louisa Banks, the sister of Isabella, appeared at the bigamy trial and said, 'I see the name of Isabella Banks to the entry in the book before me – that is the handwriting of my murdered sister.'

11

The Wyberton Murder 1860

In 1920, the writer W. J. Rawnsley, in his book on Lincolnshire, could find only one thing to say about the village of Wyberton near Boston. He talked about what might have been if the church there 'had been built as planned. It had been restored by Gilbert Scott in 1881. But that is mainline history, the kind of thing that guidebooks keep to. The real interest history has in that village is of a killing – the violent death of a police constable.'

On 24 October 1860, Constable Alexander McBrian was going about his duty when he was confronted by a man with a gun. We will never be entirely clear how and why a shot was fired but it was, and it wounded the police officer. The gunman ran off in panic. Then, at six in the morning, the Rev. Charles Moore was woken up by the barking of a dog and went out to see what was happening. He met PC McBrian, staggering and in pain, with severe bleeding from one arm. The officer said, 'I am dying for want of help ... I have been shot.' The gunman had been just four feet away when the shot was fired and poor McBrian was in a sorry state; he begged for a doctor to be called.

Another officer, Edward Crawford, was drinking at the Crown and Anchor pub on the night of the shooting and he recalled a labourer named Richardson being drunk as he left the place; the suspicions turned to this man as the injured McBrian was placed in a cart by the vicar and sent to a doctor immediately. He was to linger for a week before he died, having had the attention of two local doctors and another doctor who came from Lincoln. But the suspected man, Thomas Richardson, was examined at the Boston Sessions House on the morning after the shooting; the Chief Constable for Lincolnshire, Philip Bicknell, had been quick to examine the scene of the shooting and he had found some newspaper (*The Times* for 27 March, 1854) which had been used for wadding in a gun. Richardson said that he was innocent of the shooting.

McBrian died on 1 November, but before he died he made a statement in the presence of Richardson and a magistrate. *The Morning Chronicle* reported the scene: 'Richardson was twice taken to see the constable, and on each occasion McBrian said, "That's the man who shot me".' After the death, there was a coroner's inquest held at the Ship Inn before Mr Little, and the story of the fateful encounter came out.

Superintendent Manton told the court that McBrian had been on duty in Wyberton and Frampton that night and that when the injury was discovered, the Superintendent had sent for Dr Young nearby; McBrian was able to give an account of the events at the time. He said that he was walking near the churchyard early in the morning when he saw a man ahead who shied off the path, so he called out, 'Hello mate, where are you for?' He saw the gun and asked, 'What are you going to do with that thing?' The man said nothing, but pulled his cap down and in the words of the constable, 'fired some slap at me.' He then ran off towards Wyberton. Manton gave the story he had heard from McBrian in some detail.

Manton went to Richardson's house the next day with a sergeant and there they found a double-barrelled shotgun which had been recently fired. The sergeant fired a shot into the ground and the wadding was taken. Manton had found a scrap of newspaper at the scene of the crime and the two pieces matched. The accused said that he used wadding from brown paper, so a lie seemed evident. When asked about the events of that night Richardson said that he left the Crown and Anchor about midnight ad then met two other men, James Burrill and Thomas King; he was trying to establish an alibi, of course. But Manton went away with some shot and then he compared this with the shot in the coat of McBrian and found that they matched. When he returned to see Richardson, he charged and arrested him.

When McBrian identified Richardson he said, 'I should not have said so if it were not true, and if I am a dying man, he is the man who shot me.' Clearly, people who had noted the officer's description – admittedly spoken from sketchy evidence as it was a moonlit scene with plenty of shadow on that night – confirmed that the descriptions matched Richardson.

The witnesses at the inquest spoke also. Burrill said that he was drinking that night with Richardson and had seen him walk home and go into his house; he said that they were both 'a little fresh' after the drinking, and that he had heard someone go upstairs 'with a heavy tread' after they parted. He was perhaps trying to suggest that his friend must be innocent, as he had retired to bed, a little drunk, ready to sleep it off. But John King told a different tale, saying that he had gone home and after unlacing his boots, he had heard a shot. He said, 'I don't think Richardson would have had time to go to his house for his gun before I heard the shot …'

Of course, this statement is at odds with Manton's report that the gun was still warm early the next morning. If the shot had been fired around five o'clock, then that would make sense.

Dr Alan Young described events, and stated that when he came to attend to McBrian he saw a severe gunshot wound in his right arm, between the shoulder and the elbow. He said that the officer was suffering from extreme loss of blood and a shock to the nervous system. He also confirmed that the shot must have been fired at close range: 'There was a large orifice, showing that the shot had entered in a mass.' The cause of death was 'effusion into the chest and pericardium.' The lungs were also very congested. The man had heroically fought for his life and made sure that he had pointed out the killer before witnesses.

Dr Adam from Boston said that McBrian had told him that there was bright moonlight and there had been enough light for him to see the gunman, so that made the first statements on the killer's identity more convincing. The hearing was adjourned, and McBrian was buried in Skirbeck churchyard.

At Lincoln assizes, the evidence of the wadding and McBrian's identification were bound to win the day for the crown, and it took the jury a mere fifteen minutes to return a verdict of guilty on the indictment of murder. The sentence o death was passed and one report noted that: 'The prisoner was throughout the trial totally unmoved, and received his sentence in the most unconcerned manner possible.' This was on 5 December but there was a recommendation for a respite and, on 20 December, Mr Banks Stanhope questioned the good sense of commuting the sentence to penal servitude, asking in the House, 'Is it the case that Thomas Richardson, who was convicted at the Winter Assizes at Lincoln of the wilful murder of Police Constable McBrian, there being, in the opinion of the judge, no extenuating circumstances, and no provocation, had his sentence commuted …?' He pointed out what kind of message this was sending to those desperate types who carry firearms and who might be confronted by an officer of the law. He pointed out that another constable had been fired at since that killing.

A solitary cell from the mid Victorian years.

The Home Secretary, Sir George Lewis, said that this was not a case of premeditation. He said that the gun had been thrown down, not fired with intent to maim or kill. Strong representations had been made to him on behalf of Richardson, and Lewis said that 'There was a petition for a remission of the sentence from Boston, in the neighbourhood where the offence occurred, stating that the act was not one of deliberate murder, and that Richardson had resided at Wyberton for twenty years and was generally regarded as a very industrious man.' The petition had been signed by the Rector of the village and by several magistrates; not long after a similar petition was conceived at Lincoln. There was indeed a commutation to penal servitude for life.

The chief constable of the county submitted a report a month after the respite of the sentence, agreeing with Banks Stanhope, and arguing that the killing of a police officer should be subject to the extreme penalty of the law, and he pointed out that since the killing a stone had been thrown and a loaded gun with shot fired through the window of the house of a constable.

On Christmas Eve, 1860, the report in the press was simple and brief: 'The sentence of death passed upon Thomas Richardson at the last Lincoln Assizes for the murder of a police officer has been respited during Her Majesty's Pleasure. It appears that the deceased officer was entirely unknown to the prisoner, who could have borne him no ill will, and that the fatal shot was fired at the impulse of the moment, probably without any intention of destroying life.' (*The Times* December 24)

Richardson was transported for life to Western Australia in 1862, on board the *Norwood*. The assize record simply has one sentence under the 'other remarks' heading: 'Able to read and write imperfectly.' We have to reflect on the repercussions of this for his wife and family, but that is the dark, unknown shadow narrative of crime history.

12

Epilepsy Saved his Neck 1876

The Lincolnshire police force was formed in January, 1857, with manpower of 207 officers led by Capt. Philip Bicknell. Before that time and indeed well after its formation the everyday police work in the remote villages of the county were supervised by parish constables. The small village of Hemingby, near Horncastle, has the dubious distinction of being the place where the last parish constable was murdered. This story of the killing of Constable Thomas Bett Gell is notable for two reasons; it took place in an area that had a unique local history of policing, and it involved a classic narrative of the Victorian criminal justice system when it came to understand insanity.

The victim was a parish constable, an office with a very long history. In the reign of Edward I a law was made placing two constables in each parish, though this was not eagerly enforced; then, in 1285, the Statute of Westminster began the 'watch and ward' approach to crime patrolling; basically, a night watchman who was to be alert late at night and in the early hours. But by the mid-Victorian period, rural areas still presented a tough problem for the local forces of law and order.

As research by historian B. J. Davey has shown, Horncastle had a most interesting policing structure in the years between 1838 and 1857. Because of an obscure Act of Parliament, the Lighting and Watching Act of 1833, the town in the Lincolnshire Wolds organised and paid its own constabulary. A young lawyer, Richard Clitherow, kept detailed records of the police functions and of crimes for almost twenty years, and we have a rich understanding of the nature of crime in the town.

Just before policing was revolutionised in 1857, Bicknell took up the post of Chief Constable; he was the one Chief Constable for the county, but the ultimate aim was to have one person in that office for each area. A fundamental problem – and it was one which was to have a bearing on this case – was the fact that Bicknell could not transfer a man to another area without the officer losing his pension rights. This was not remedied until 1865.

Difficulties like these were behind the cumbersome process of having a full-time officer close to the thousands of scattered villages across Lincolnshire, to help the amateurs when needed. Bicknell, who retired in 1902, was the man most responsible for improving the police administration in the county, but his efforts came too late for the constable of tiny Hemingby.

The constable featured in this story had been selected according to Bicknell's requirements. When he looked for a constable for the force he was anxious to recruit the right kind of man; his criteria was principally that the man should be clean, active, intelligent and 'of good height and well made.' Bicknell actually wrote an instruction book, *Bicknell's Police Manual*, and in that, one of his directives was that each member of the force 'with his wife and children, is to attend service every Sunday, unless there be good reason to the contrary, and his children are to be sent to school.'

In Bicknell's long reign the Hemingby murder was one of the worst experiences he had – and that includes riots in Lincoln in 1862 and several high-profile murders. Thomas Bett Gell's death pinpointed the weaknesses of the attempts to police such a massive rural area. B. J. Davey, in his book *Lawless and Immoral* (see bibliography) which was concerned with the years shortly before the new county and borough police, makes it clear that the Horncastle force, covering Hemingby and other villages nearby, had a wide and demanding remit and a formidable range of crimes to deal with. The police notebooks Davey used for his study show that there was a very high incidence of violent crime. He says something very relevant to the Gell case that helps us understand how vulnerable and hard-pressed the constable was: ' *The people of Horncastle were usually not very worried about serious crimes like robbery and they did not expect the likes of Ackrill and Gapp [constables previous to Gell] to be able to do much about things anyway. They wanted the policeman to deal with the lawless and immoral, to reduce drunkenness, vice and considerable disorder throughout the town ...*'

Country towns always had their problems of social order and crime was often public and in the streets. While London was developing the status and workings of the first 'Peelers' after Sir Robert Peel's Police Act of 1829, and the Metropolitan Police was born, the provinces continued to cope for several decades with part-timers in the constabularies. The duties of a parish constable were onerous and included the supervision of prisoners, putting them in stocks or securing them in a lock-up, and taking them before a magistrate when the time came. He would not necessarily have a uniform and had only a wooden truncheon to symbolise his office or to instil fear. Nevertheless, the constables coped well. In 1876, when policing had been radically changed in many parts of the land, the villages clustered around Horncastle still relied on the local constable; in Hemingby, the officer was a blacksmith when he was not on duty, and of course, he was always on call in emergencies. In the 1871 census, Gell was listed as a wheelwright master employing two men and two boys. One of his fellow tradesmen was to become his killer.

What Gell was faced with when he was killed was nothing ordinary, and needed experts and a force of men to deal with it. This was not possible; Gell was alone.

On 15 October, 1876, the blacksmith William Drant, a man with a long history of violence and savage mood-swings, came home after a night of heavy drinking. His wife had left him some time before, and he was living with his mother at the time of this affair. He had brought home a family friend on the night in question. At first all was well but he began to change mood and to become loud and abusive. This happened after he had complained of feeling ill, and had been taken to the house of a Mrs Goddard for some sort of help, and then had been taken home again. At home he lay down and tried to sleep, but after half an hour he awoke and was dangerously aggressive.

Drant, thirty-seven years old and very sturdy and strong, started to rant about Mrs Goddard trying to poison him; she was extremely patient and tried her best to help him and quieten him, but he got to his feet and threatened her with his fists. From that time on his behaviour can only be called manic. *The Times* reported it in these terms: 'He then called for his mother, who, taking alarm, had run out to find assistance. He went out to fetch her and returned, dragging her by the neck into the kitchen of the house, where he flung her onto the floor, and kneeling on her, he took out a knife and threatened to murder her ...'

The situation then escalated into an open confrontation as four neighbours arrived, two carrying wooden rails from a fence. They wrestled him away from his mother and

EPILEPTIC HOMICIDE.

TO THE EDITOR OF THE TIMES.

Sir,—Will you permit me to call attention in your columns to what you justly describe as a very painful case? I would do so in the hope that such further inquiries may be made by the proper authorities as your report seems to render necessary.

At the Lincolnshire Assizes just held, William Drant was tried for the murder of Thomas Bett Gell. On the evening of the murder he had been taken ill in a neighbour's cottage; he was cold, trembled very much, and was extremely pale in the face, crying out, "O, Lord, save me!" he begged some one to pray with him, and said to his mother, "Kiss me, Jane, I'm dying!" His mother kissed him and he kissed her. When he got home he lay on the sofa, feeling very sick, and his mother pulled his boots off for him. Suddenly he jumped up, exclaiming, "There's Jane," and, without any provocation whatever, seized his mother by the neck, threw her on the floor, dragged her about by the hair, and then, kneeling on her chest and brandishing over her a knife which he had pulled out, threatened to kill her. Four men armed with bars came to the rescue, and, after striking him on the head and on the arm, disarmed him, he resisting furiously. After the struggle he was quiet for a moment, then seized one of the pieces of wood which had been thoughtlessly thrown on the floor, sprang up, suddenly rushed out of the house after the men, who fled, and, overtaking one of them, felled him with a terrific blow on the back of the head and beat in his skull with blows which sounded like "blows on an empty barrel with a lump of wood." When apprehended he was very violent, threatening to kill the first person who came near him. Afterwards, when charged with the murder, he exclaimed, "Oh, dear! Oh, dear! I did'nt think I had killed him."

The mother's evidence, which is of extreme importance in regard to the interpretation of this unprovoked outburst of homicidal fury, is as follows:—

"When my son was quite a child he suffered from fits and has very much subsequently. He had two or three fits on the Tuesday night previous to this occurrence. On the following day (Wednesday) he had four or five fits. He

Letter on Epilepsy regarding the Drant affair.

took the knife. One managed to crack Drant on the head and this almost stopped him, yet he recovered and hit back, narrowly missing one of his assailants.

The next stage was an attack on another blacksmith of the village who obviously knew him. It is not clear whether this man, Leggit, tried to appease the rabid Drant or to tackle him, but he was threatened and ran off. There was so much noise in the street by this time that Constable Gell was roused and he arrived just as Drant ran out into the street, swinging a piece of rail. He struck Gell with considerable force. One witness reported: 'It felled him to the ground and repeated blows were heard, sounding as if striking an empty barrel.' The officer was dying, his brain severely damaged. A doctor attended him, but there was no hope and he died the next morning.

While the victim was battling for life, Drant had been caught and carried off to the Horncastle lock-up, the Roundhouse, after being arrested by PC Lawson from nearby Baumber (one and a half miles away), one of the 'new police.' Drant was charged with assault and attempted murder. His only reply was a deranged one: 'They have worked me

Lincoln Hanging Suite.

up so much I couldn't stand it a minute longer, watching and peeping about my house, and I've given Gell one.' What emerged later was that Drant had once been employed by Gell, and had been sacked. There was bad blood between them and witnesses stated that Drant had spoken aggressively against Gell on several occasions. But now, in the lock-up, he began to change mood and eventually said, in a more sober tone, 'Oh dear Oh dear, I am sorry. I did not think I had killed him!' This was said as he was charged with murder at the inquest, held at the Coach and Horses pub at Hemingby, and the charge of wilful murder meant that he was on his way to the next Lincoln assizes.

The trial was on 29 December and baron Huddkleston presided. The prosecution was led by Barnard and Lumley, and the man charged with assembling some kind of defence was Horace Smith. Smith tried his best to approach the issue by way of the theory of insanity at the time, referring to the fits to which the accused was subject. Apart from that, his most relevant defence was that there was no real malice and intent to murder, so manslaughter would seem to be apposite. Smith had to rely, as every lawyer did then, on the McNaghten Rules, stating that if insanity is proven there is an absence of *mens rea*, intent to kill, and so the jury should commit the prisoner to hospital and confinement for an indefinite period. For Smith, his only basis for argument was the instance of the 'fits.' The McNaghten Rules had been laid down as recently as 1844, and the crucially important words were, 'the accused ... at the time of committing the act, must have been labouring under such defect of reason, from disease of the mind, as not to know the nature and quality of the act.' The formative event here was the murder of Sir Robert Peel's private secretary in 1843; the proceedings were halted over a plea of insanity.

In the middle years of the nineteenth century there was a steady realisation that the new science of psychology would play a part in the forensics of crime. The issue of who was bad and who was mad had become, by the 1850s, something demanding debate. A number of medical men working in asylums or in universities began to identify varieties of insanity and distinguish them from such behaviour as epileptic fits. None of this knowledge was likely to be applied in this murder case from remote Lincolnshire.

This was because Huddleston saw no problem at all with Drant's behaviour and general condition. His words were: 'The law presumed all killing to be murder and it rested upon the accused to show that the offence was manslaughter only.' Amazingly, he spoke directly to the jury in his summing-up and directed not to take 'a cowardly refuge' in either alternative (manslaughter or insanity) to avoid responsibility. To be fair, he instructed them with reference to the McNaghten Rules but then led the summary into a recounting of the accused's actions on the fateful day.

Drant, he reminded them, had been subject to no provocation from Gell in terms of an attempt to stop him injuring his mother. He did admit that Drant had had a violent blow to the back of his head, and that 'this had confused him' and, rather unexpectedly, opened up the possibility of an escape from the murder charge: 'The accused snatched up the first weapon near him and so caused the death of the deceased ... the offence might be manslaughter ...' The jury took twenty-five minutes to decide that Drant was guilty of murder.

On 7 December, a major figure in the new psychology of deviance wrote a letter to *The Times* about the case. This was Henry Maudsley, a man who was totally preoccupied with the debate on what was then called 'degeneration' – an off-shoot of Darwinian evolution – which was concerned with understanding criminality in terms of genetic and physiological traits. Maudsley was interested in the epilepsy alleged to be in Drant's medical profile. Maudsley drew attention to the condition of Drant before the onset of the violence: 'On the evening of the murder he had been taken ill in a neighbour's cottage; he was cold, trembled very much and was extremely pale in the face, crying out "Oh Lord save me!"' Maudsley had reflected on the progress of the outburst, read between the lines, and seen a familiar pattern of epileptic symptoms. Arguably, informed public opinion must have been affected by such a prominent medical man writing to the *Thunderer* about the affair. His lengthy, detailed letter, expressed with care and precision, must have alarmed the legal professionals who had experienced such behaviour in previous cases. That such a respected doctor even noticed an obscure killing was also notably rare.

Maudsley then noted that the most useful information about the illness came from Drant's mother. She had said that her son had had fits since he was a child, and that he had had two such seizures on the Tuesday before the killing, and 'four or five' again on the Wednesday. She went on: 'He usually went violent after these fits. During the time he was in the house on the fateful night he was talking to himself. I washed him about seven o'clock when he was trembling violently and seemed to know nothing.' Quite rightly, Maudsley was acute enough to realise that the person closest to the killer, his mother, was well informed about the 'case history' and in fact expressed the symptoms and habits of the poor victim of the illness very ably and accurately. Once again, we have a Victorian murder trial in which the medical discourse available is very limited and mostly unheard.

Mrs Drant said that the local doctor, Boulton, had attended William several times recently and that a few days before the incident she had slept with her bedroom door open for fear of her son's likely sudden fit of rage or distraction. All this was just what Maudsley needed to confirm an opinion that should have found a place in the trial, and he wrote that such behaviour was 'epileptic mania ... well know to have most furious and dangerous consequences.' His description of the condition certainly fits Drant's case; he was described as, 'Sane enough, perhaps, and even amiable, industrious and well-behaved during the fits, then these unfortunate persons become immediately after them most violent and destructive beings for a time ... and when they come to themselves they are utterly unconscious of what they have done in their state of alienation.' The doctor had seen the significance of the pattern of Drant's actions and suffering, and seen them as a template, a defining sequence of manifestations of the illness.

Perhaps Maudsley caught the real mood of the Hemingby people after the trial, because he put on his academic tone and said that if a lecturer were to be given a case study of Drant he would not be able to quote 'a more typical example than the painful case of William Drant who is now lying under sentence of death.' Drant's neighbours and fellow citizens petitioned the Home Office, asking for a reprieve, and it was granted. He was detained 'during Her Majesty's Pleasure.'

It was *The Times* reporter who had called this 'a painful case,' and it is a fitting description. As for the victim, Constable Gell, he was buried in the churchyard at Hemingby, surely respected and admired by his friends and clients.

Maudsley, who had played a part in helping the case to a satisfactory conclusion, went on to found a centre for research into mental illness, a happy departure from the normal practice of setting up yet another asylum. Ironically, only a short distance from Hemingby, the Lincoln Bracebridge asylum had, by 1890, almost a thousand patients inside its dour walls. Sadly for Drant, there is no doubt that he faced a future in which his epileptic attacks would take place in very unpleasant circumstances, although there would be caring professionals looking after him.

There had been other deaths besides Gell's in the line of duty in the new police and acts of heroism; only three years before this homicide, PC Tidbury had received a medal for gallantry for jumping from a moving train to recapture a prisoner. Two years after the Hemingby drama PC Little had rescued a lady 'from a most perilous position' on a rooftop. The Albert medal was created in 1866, and preceded what was to become the King's Police medal in 1909. Unfortunately there was no such award for Gell; there will never be anything 'heroic' about running across town and meeting a crazed man in a homicidal fit, but somehow we have to feel that Gell deserves more than an honourable gravestone. Maybe this story, retelling those tragic events, will encourage people to think again about the more routine deaths in police history.

13

Mrs Maybrick 1889

In the nineteenth century, the ubiquity of fly-papers in the average home was something that could lead from routine habits to a suggestion of heinous foul play. They were a neat way to rid the house of insects, but when they were soaked, for arsenic to be extracted for other uses, there could be trouble. In Battlecrease House, in Augburth, this was a factor in the puzzling and desperately sad story of Florence Maybrick. To make matters worse for her, she was married to a man who enjoyed taking tiny quantities of poison, for all kinds of reasons.

When that man, James Maybrick, died, the finger of guilt pointed at his wife. The story went on to become not only a famous and controversial case, but a story that has been acquired by the vast library of Jack the Ripper theories, as James was in the habit of visiting London, and his strange personality gave rise to a certain line of enquiry about him.

The story of the Maybricks began when James was on board the liner, Baltic, in 1880. There he met young Florence, only eighteen at the time, and Maybrick was forty-two. Florence had been born in Mobile, Alabama; her mother aspired to wealth and status and wanted the same for her daughter. Mrs Maybrick's third husband had been a German aristocrat, and so the American lady was actually no less than the Baroness von Roques if she wanted to pull rank or put on airs. James Maybrick, along with many other men, found Florence to be very alluring. She was an attractive blonde, blue-eyed and very shapely. It must have been a stunning contrast for her when they married and moved to Liverpool, after living first in Norfolk, Virginia, for a while.

After they married in 1881, they settled at Battlecrease House in Aigburth; the place is a huge building, and Maybrick had acquired considerable wealth in the cotton business. But the change in lifestyle and cultural ambience must have been depressing for the young bride. She was a product of the American South, and of the wealthy, socialising element of that culture. Now she was in a British suburb of a fast-growing industrial city with a very sombre and grey climate. Society and social gatherings were limited for her, and her husband was often away from home.

They had children, and on the surface at least they would have appeared to be like every other middle class couple. But the main problem lay with James. As time went on, his business floundered. Not only was he failing in commerce, but in his personality he was nurturing habits that would ruin his health. Maybrick was drawn to the questionable pleasures of taking poisons and drugs to keep an edge on life (in fact to enhance sexual potency, as arsenic was taken to do). He also lived the fairly typical double life of the Victorian married man; attentive husband at home but malcontented womaniser when he could find the time and opportunity.

Clearly, Florence would soon find the stress of this relationship, and the loneliness it imposed on her, too much to handle. The fact that Maybrick then set about saving money at home by imposing privations and discipline on the domestic routine was perhaps the last straw. She wrote to her mother (living in Paris at the time) that she was in a mood to leave the house and move elsewhere, and doubted that 'life was worth living', things were so bad. Her situation was ripe for the relief, pleasure and fulfilment that an affair would bring. She found the man in Alfred Brierley, a man in the same line of business as James.

Her mistake, as we look on her life with the knowledge of hindsight, was that she was not discrete. She and Brierley would have times together in London posing as a married couple. But her strains at the hands of Maybrick were intolerable. He had a mistress, and she equally became rash about her attempts to find pleasure outside marriage. There was an element of torment in their relationship, even to the point of Florence flirting with James's brother, Edwin. Things were moving towards some kind of crisis; they were not sleeping together, and Florence was thinking about leaving him.

At this point, enter the fly-papers. Because she was in the habit of using a mixture of arsenic and elderflower to treat boils on her face, the soaking papers were a common sight in the house. But then James's illness came. On 27 April, he was ill and he blamed this on a prescription of strychnine being wrongly calculated. This would have made sense to a man with those strange habits of pleasure. But his health began to decline more severely. Fate was stacking the odds against Florence, as the servants were noticing the soaking fly-papers and linking that to their master's decline. After all, he had cut her from his will and had been insulting and aggressive towards her on many occasions. She had cause to detest him. The illness dragged on, and a nurse was employed to be with the patient at all times.

Maybrick's brother, Edwin, also came, and he took charge of things. The situation then was that Florence was estranged from her man; she was seen as a potentially deranged woman with a grudge against her husband, and there was evidence mounting against her with regard to the arsenic. Even worse, bearing in mind the morality of the time, she wrote to her lover, Brierley, trying to arrange a meeting with him before he left the country; in that letter she referred to Maybrick's condition and noted that he had no suspicion of the affair. Florence was often present at the sick man's bedside and unfortunately for her, she played a part in using the medicines, saying that James had actually asked her to give him some arsenic in powder form. Everything she seemed to do in the role of nurse or caring wife turned into facts to be used against her when Maybrick died, as he did on 11 May. She was arrested on suspicion of wilful murder, by Superintendent Bryning.

The high drama continued even to the point of her mother entering the scene, there was a confrontation and Florence put the situation very neatly, saying to her, 'They think I poisoned Jim.' She was taken first to Lark Lane station, and then to Walton gaol.

The trial began at St George's Hall on 31 July, and Sir Charles Russell led her defence. There was great confusion in the forensic and medical evidence, even to the point of two experts disagreeing about whether or not the deceased had died from arsenical poisoning. Events went against her, and in the end it could be said that Florence was a victim of the judge. This is because there was just so much testimony about Maybrick's habits of pumping his body full of drugs and poisons that he was dicing with death anyway, and ruining his health for many years before these suspicions were first aroused about his wife's alleged designs on him. The judge, Mr Justice Fitzjames Stephen, directed his long summing-up to the likely guilt of Florence if certain facts were ignored; that is, he reinforced the accusations of moral lapses against her, to the detriment of the actual issue of murder. He was ludicrously biased in his dramatic account of the situation of slow poison on a supposed 'loved one.' Naturally, the jury would begin to turn against Florence and forget the contradictions about the actual nature and administering of the poison. Arguably, the judge's action which had the most impact on the jury was his mention

Cover for an early booklet on
the Maybrick murder,

of the letter to Brierley about Maybrick being 'sick unto death' and his very evident repugnance at what he was implying she had done and written with such callousness. The jury surely must have been influenced by seeing this. There was definitely 'reasonable doubt' in the case, and a death sentence was outrageous. Yet, on 7 August, Florence Maybrick was sentenced to hang. The judge, leaving the court, was the target of general public abuse and displeasure, so wrong was his sentence perceived to be.

The real heart of this sensational trial was Florence's loud assertion that she was innocent of this crime: 'I was guilty of intimacy with Mr Brierley, but I am not guilty of this crime.'

But the real sensation was yet to come, after the death sentence was passed on her. There was a strong and widespread campaign for clemency, and this was going on even at the time that Florence was awaiting her fate in Walton prison (with gallows being made ready outside). The Home Secretary arranged a reprieve; the sentence was to be commuted to penal servitude for life. But in 1904 she was released and returned to America. There, as the writer Richard Whittington-Egan has written, she hid herself away in the Berkshire foothills; she became 'Florence Chandler' in South Kent, Connecticut. The person who became the epitome of the dotty and lonely old spinster, surrounded by cats, as Whittington-Egan says, 'was known to successive generations of South Kent boys as *The Cat Woman*.' She died in 1941, aged eighty-one. History tells of two Florence Maybricks, then, but there is another – the lonely prisoner, unjustly incarcerated, in those silent years before release.

History has leaned to the view that gastroenteritis, not murder, led to Maybrick's death.

14

Dr Whitmarsh 1898

The term 'back street abortion' suggests a seedy quack doctor working in a poor district of some urban sprawl, treating poor desperate women with half-baked and dangerous methods of intrusive medical work. The case of John Lloyd Whitmarsh matches that very well, except for one detail; his premises were in Brompton Road. One might have expected a rather more progressive and educated clientele, but the fact is that this man was a very dangerous character. In 1898, he found himself facing a charge of murder.

The story is really a sad one, one of thousands of similar stories about 'women in trouble' down the ages; in this instance, it was Alice Bayly, who worked as a saleswoman at a drapery shop in Woolwich. Alice started walking out with a man called Edward de Nobrega, a married man and a womaniser, as it turned out. Nobrega's wife, Annie, first heard of her husband's mistress when a parcel arrived at her house addressed to a 'Mr Noble.' The parcel contained some bottles; the name and address of the sender were on the parcel, so Annie went to see her in Woolwich. She learned there what she thought to be the truth, that Noble and Nobrega were the same man – her husband.

Alice Bayly first met Nobrega in Molesey five years before these events; the two women had a tearful meeting, and the wife asked outright: 'Is there anything to be ashamed of in your friendship?' Alice broke down, but she never said that she was pregnant, merely going on to say that she had not known the man was married and that she would never willingly see Nobrega again. Annie left and the two never met again. Nobrega and Annie had been married for twelve years and had three children; it was a common situation in Victorian marriages, the husband often having a mistress or looking for sex with prostitutes, but this time the business was to lead to tragedy. Alice Bayly and Nobrega had decided that an abortion was the answer to her pregnancy, and the bottles in question were a prepared medicine by Dr Whitmarsh, containing mercury. Alice had died following a visit to Whitmarsh, and the death and been slow and agonisingly painful. The poor woman, just 26 years old, had died at Charing Cross Hospital on the 10 July.

Alice's mother told the story at the inquest where Mr John Troutbeck presided; Whitmarsh was being investigated with regard to a possible case of performing an illegal operation upon the deceased. Her daughter's health was normally very good, but she had started walking out with Nobrega for some years, and on June 19 in this year, she saw that Alice was ill. There were pains in her joints and she was sick; Dr Clarke of Plumstead (where they lived) came and thought the problem was rheumatic fever. Alice felt better on the following day but then there was a relapse. A day later she was very ill again, and she said to her mother: 'The old man done it.' She then said that she had burned the letters, and began to weep and sob, saying that she had 'gone wrong.'

Obviously, the mother pressed Alice on the identity of the old man in question, and the young woman wrote the name and address on some paper; there was another daughter in the family, called Laura, and she sent a telegram to the address given. They urgently needed to see this medical man, whoever he was. Eventually, after there was no reply, Alice begged her sister to go to the address and tell the old man to come. She said, 'I am dying … he has done it and he must come and see what he can do for me …' At first he did not come, but then, after another day had passed with Alice's terrible suffering, he did come.

Whitmarsh came to the sick woman, who told him that he had killed her, but his only reply was that she would be all right in a day or two. Her mouth was ulcerated, and she showed him that; it was noted by the family that the doctor smelled of alcohol, and he merely said that he would call again. When he returned, he was worried. Alice said, 'Oh doctor what have you done to me?' Even then, all he could do was give directions for a certain type of poultice to be prepared and then he left.

Two other doctors were called and Alice was taken to hospital. Before she died, Alice told her mother that she had had a miscarriage; a letter had arrived at their house that week, and it was from Nobrega. He wrote: 'All my thoughts are with you, and if I do not suffer physically like yourself, I do so mentally. I sincerely trust soon to learn that you are getting on towards recovery. If you think I can do anything to alleviate your suffering or to ease your mind, do let me know through your sister, who was very kind to me when I saw her on Thursday.'

It was a tragic tale. After her death only a few pawn tickets were found on her; she earned £50 a year working in retail, and never saved any money. The abortion had, of course, been arranged and paid for by Nobrega. She wrote a note in reply to the letter, asking Edmund Nobrega to come and see her.

Laura gave testimony, and told of her visit to Whitmarsh; he had ignored the telegram, which was lying on a table when she arrived at his house. He eventually opened it and thought that as Plumstead was a long way, it was not necessary to go, and he knew that other doctors would be attending to Alice. Laura then met with Nobrega, and at that meeting he said he had never heard of a Dr Whitmarsh; Alice heard of this and said, 'Oh he won't own up to that' and she said how she had come to know that he was a liar. Not long before, Alice had asked Laura to lend her £4 but had not said what she needed the money for. But she had been for the abortion, and had found the money somehow; Nobrega later admitted that he had seen Alice looking very ill, and had given her a sovereign to pay Whitmarsh. They had all had enough of the quack by this point and two telegrams were sent to him, telling him to stay away.

Other people who knew Alice gave their comments. Louie Dale, who had worked with her, said that she had seen Alice in great pain but she had still continued serving customers, and when Louie asked what was wrong she just said that she had been into the city with her mother and it had 'knocked her up.' Ellen West, who also worked in the shop, had known Alice for six years and had shared a flat with her. She recalled Alice receiving a bottle of medicine through the post, and that it had been broken. She had heard Alice say, 'That fool of a man has sent me some medicine through the post and it has got broken. When I was in the city on Thursday I had a bad headache and he said he had something to help.' This all seemed like a plausible cover-up tale. The witness did remember references to a doctor living in London at Brompton Road but she had never heard anything of Nobrega taking Alice to a chemist.

Flora Horsfall, another millinery assistant, said that she found Alice in bed, complaining of severe abdominal pains. Flora was asked to go to the shop and collect the largest bath towel available. After that, Alice had said she would be all right, but the day after she showed Flora her mouth: 'Her teeth were black and her gums of a brownish colour', Flora said, and apparently Alice had said, 'Oh Miss Horsford, surely I have not been poisoned!' She told Flora that she had 'had a draught' in London the day before. Owen Dale, who owned the shop, was naturally very concerned for his employee's welfare, and she commented that he thought she had been anaemic for some time; he had given her three weeks' leave on the previous occasion of her illness (after the miscarriage).

Attending that coroner's inquest was the famous detective Drew, the man who was to be notorious for his work on the Dr Crippen case in 1910. In this instance, he was simply stating what actions were being taken to link these matters to Whitmarsh; he said there had been no label on the broken bottle but that enquiries were being made.

The Westminster Coroner's Court was certainly a focus for press attention by this time; poisoning cases and anything underhand such as illegal operations were, of course, good material for scandal. Attention now turned more closely to Nobrega. This was of special interest because it was now known that Alice had had a miscarriage almost a year before the taking of the medicine from Whitmarsh. The legal advisers for Nobrega had this put aside while forensic matters were discussed. Dr Thomas Stevenson from Guy's Hospital described the pathology. He only found one poisonous material present in the viscera: mercury. The key point in his extensive account of the condition of the organs was that there was nothing to indicate how the mercury was introduced into the body. The facts, he said, did seem to indicate that the mercury was administered in some other way, than by mouth. The poison was present in the liver, kidneys and elsewhere.

Dr Stevenson said that, if given in the right way, such treatment and such amounts indicated nothing unusual. But the references to the bottles, the ulcerated gums and the mercury in the organs suggested that Whitmarsh needed to stand trial in court. Inspector Drew had actually had a model made of Whitmarsh's rooms made by PC Greenwood of M Division. All agreed that this matched the statements given by Laura Ivory, Alice's sister. Surely, only fine details – matters pertaining to the place as a surgery for abortion practice – would be relevant, and, although the first reports do not specify this, it must arguably have been Drew's intention in supplying the model.

Nobrega had not been called, so everyone had to wait for more details on his involvement, but the coroner concluded by summing up the reasons why the case had to proceed to criminal trial:

'If they were of the opinion that the deceased died by mercurial poisoning, they must say if that was due to an illegal action. The suggestion was that it was due to an illegal action, viz. the endeavour to procure an abortion. The procuration of an abortion was an illegal action and if death occurred as a direct consequence of a felony, it was laid down in the law that it was murder.'

The jury had to decide if there had been such an attempt, and if that action was the cause of the death. The coroner reminded the jury that Alice had called Nobrega 'a wicked liar.'

More substance was given to Nobrega's very unpleasant character when it emerged that, as Alice lay dying in hospital, he had remonstrated with her about her previous miscarriage and how she had not learned her lesson. But, in the end, it was said by Alice before she died that Whitmarsh had operated on her, and so, in spite of other parties all playing their part in this tragedy – including, as the coroner pointed out, the editors of journals in which advertisements were placed for these dreadful services – it was Whitmarsh who was to stand trial for murder. Whitmarsh had agreed to do the operation for £4, in his surgery over a baker's shop in Brompton Road. Laura Ivory had said in court that she overheard a conversation at Whitmarsh's place, and after Laura had said she heard a man's voice say, 'It must come away ... I am not going to risk my neck on the gallows for you or anyone else,' the questioning went like this:

Mr Grain (prosecuting Whitmarsh): 'You were not listening – it came upon you by surprise?'
Laura: 'Yes, it quite frightened me.'
Mr Grain: 'You heard it involuntarily, as it were?'
Laura: 'Yes, I heard Dr Whitmarsh say what I have said, quite distinctly.'

The sheer revulsion felt by anyone hearing the details of the 'operation' must always be felt in this kind of context. Alice had told Dr Clarke when he attended her that she had kept something back from him: 'On Saturday I had a miscarriage. I was eight weeks pregnant ... I went to town and a man passed an instrument ... I came home and the miscarriage took place.' Inspector Drew had been to talk to her in Charing Cross Hospital and she confessed to him that she had, in desperation when pregnant on the first occasion, also taken various other substances, saying, 'I have been on intimate terms with a man whose name I do not wish to disclose ... I found myself pregnant and took other pills, I also took some Epsom Salts and some gin. It did not have the desired effect.'

Alice then described Whitmarsh and the circumstances of the operation. She had paid him £4 in gold and he had taken her behind some curtains and a screen in his rooms. The mysterious doctor was then described, so we have our first visual glimpse of the shadowy figure. Drew summarised her account: 'Whitmarsh is about 70 years of age, height about 5ft 6in. with rather grey hair and a moustache.'

Alice gave a dying declaration and Inspector Drew guided her towards saying the words that would have guaranteed the next stage of the prosecution. That was at the Old Bailey, and as well as the repetition of all the facts as heard by the coroner, there is another memoir of the end of that trial, and that is by the journalist Robert Watson, who wrote:

'At the October sessions of the Old Bailey, '98, I was present when three men were sentenced to death, two on one day. Dr John Lloyd Whitmarsh was indicted for the murder of Alice Bayly by performing an illegal operation. There was a marvelous difference between the doctors when on trial. Dr William Mansell Collins wept, mourned and fainted and finally, when sentence was pronounced, was carried down the steps of the dock ...'

But there was something remarkable about this case, above and beyond the actual horrendous events: it was the first time that a prisoner, charged with a capital offence, was able to give evidence; the Act allowing that came in this year. In fact, as Watson wrote, 'No man ever stood in the dock on trial for his life more stolidly indifferent to his fate.' The full horror of his treatment came out; mercury that was administered in the vagina rather than the mouth.

The jury was in confusion and disagreement; at first, they had only one in favour of an acquittal, who thought that the woman was guiltier than the man. When the time for an announcement came, it was thought by some that a manslaughter verdict would be reached but Mr Justice Bingham, presiding, directed with regard to murder, and that such a verdict was the only one possible if the evidence was believed. Bingham said, 'There is no defence in this case ... now consider your verdict and be quick about it ...'

Watson wrote that he had a friend who told him that Whitmarsh wrote of Holloway where he had been kept on remand as 'a living hell.' It was thought that he would get a seven year sentence. But with Bingham's words in mind that was looking like a bleak prospect, and Watson reported the closing words:

'Whitmarsh, in answer to the question put by Mr Avory, the Clerk of the Court, "Have you anything to say why sentence should not be passed upon you according to the law," said snappishly and contemptuously, "No." It was the first death sentence the judge had passed and he read the grim formula from a book. Whitmarsh passed hurriedly down the steps of the dock as if he had been a free man ...'

But the reprieve for Whitmarsh was received at Holloway. The old rhyme applied, as the reprieve came quickly: 'All that I ask is a short reprieve/till I forget to love and learn to grieve.' *The Times* announced the plain facts: 'The Governor of Holloway prison has received the official documents committing Dr Whitmarsh, who was recently sentenced to death at the Old Bailey, to penal servitude for life. Dr Whitmarsh ... will now be removed to Wormwood Scrubs prison to undergo the probationary part of his sentence.'

If we look for ironies and special insights into the sidelights of criminal history, we find them here, in popular culture. There was a poem around at this time called *The Shop Girl*, and it had these lines:

'When I came to the shop some years ago
I was terribly shy and simple;
With my skirt too high and my hat too low
And an unbecoming dimple.
But soon I learnt with a customer's aid
How men make up to a sweet little maid;
And another lesson I've learnt since then,
How a dear little maid 'makes up' to men.

Alice Bayly, one of this group of vulnerable young women, caught in a sense 'between classes' and open to the enthralling dreams of fantasy about transmuting into glamorous lifestyles, 'walking out' with older men and having parties and afternoon tea, was one who saw this fade into horrendous suffering and tragedy.

15

The Horace Rayner Story 1907

In 1907, the great barrister, Sir Edward Marshall Hall, was asked by the *Daily Mail* to write to Lord Alverstone about the case of a young man called Raynor who had shot dead the millionaire shop-owner, William Whiteley. Consumerism and mass media were then, after their steadily increasing influence in criminal matters in the last century, beginning to think that they could even save a neck.

It was to be the beginning of the closure of a remarkable case which had every worker in Britain greedy for the next snippet of news about Rayner, the 'youthful assassin.' In one sense, this story is a continuation of the last chapter; for once again we have, at its core, the ongoing narrative of corruption and exploitation involving rich businessmen and poor shop girls.

The tale begins with the life of William Whiteley. He was born in Yorkshire in 1831, the eldest son of a corn factory worker who left him to the care of his uncle, where he was a draper's apprentice in Wakefield. But it would be hard to find a more classic and glittering example of the product of the 'self help' ideology that percolated into Victorian Britain. At just twenty years of age, he went to the Great Exhibition, and there is no doubt that this marvellous display of goods, skills and trades inspired him to become something important, to live on a grand scale. He was determined to make a fortune and a reputation. Almost in folk-tale fashion, Whiteley went down to London after he had established what we would now call networking contacts. He had £5 on him and he was looking for investment openings. At first he worked for a company called Willey on Ludgate Hill, learning the retail trade; he was watching and learning.

He found exactly that in a part of London which was known as 'Bankruptcy Avenue' – Westbourne Grove in Bayswater. Companies had failed and it was a matter of low rents and desperate people. It would be a cheap place to open his first draper's shop and that is exactly what he did, having a rent of just £150 a year. But his best ploy was to make sure he did not join the failures by now allowing credit; he even managed to sell at very low prices and so helped other firms to go under. But his talents went further, because he knew about customer service, the psychology of retail and the value of 'PR.'

He soon progressed and after a year or so he employed fifteen people. A few years later he had a chain of shops – ten in the same area. But he expanded from drapery into any version of retail, being a forerunner of the Harrods's reputation for obtaining anything. He actually procured an elephant for one client. He was the template of the shifting, adaptable and creative entrepreneur, even fitting out some African dignitaries on a visit to the Queen with capes suitable for the occasion. He made enemies but expanded immensely and did everything the successful tycoon did then, including keeping a mistress and having passions and hobbies; but his marriage failed and he was left to have fun living a bachelor life.

By 1890 Whiteley had over 6,000 employees, and many were living in places he owned; but his empire included manufacture and supply as well as the outlets, because

The condemned cell at Newgate.

he also bought farmland and established food-processing plants. His success was acknowledged by the Queen when he was awarded a Royal Warrant, meaning he would supply certain goods to the household, in 1896.

In this lifestyle lay the kernel of his death, because he and his mistress, Louie Turner, would often have jaunts with her sister and her husband. This latter couple, Emily and George, had a son called Horace, and this young man was deranged and existing in a fantasy world in which he had taken the possibility that his father was actually William Whiteley and he began to be in all important ways, a persona called Cecil Whiteley, son of the great man who was famed as the 'Universal provider' in the retail world.

Then, in January, 1907, Horace Rayner/Cecil Whiteley, deranged and dangerous, went to ask Whiteley for money; when this request was refused, Rayner shot Whiteley twice at point blank range and then tried to kill himself but failed. In the suicide attempt he lost an eye.

So it was that the one-eyed Horace sat in court at the Old Bailey on 22 March; the trial lasted five hours and after just twenty minutes the jury found him guilty of murder. The only possibility of a reprieve was on the grounds of his mental instability, but of course, he had a clear intention to kill, and the attempt on his own life was also a crime and he was indicted for that. It was virtually a miracle that he did survive the attempt on his own life. One report was that '… but for the great skill of the surgeons Rayner would have died from the injuries he inflicted upon himself the instant after the murder.' He had shot out one eye with the revolver and in court he had a glass eye; as *The New York Times* reported: 'It shocks a large section of the British public to think that Rayner's life was saved simply that he might be put to death by the hangman.'

The public were indeed concerned; the press led the crusade for a reprieve, and hundreds of thousands of people signed a petition. The general feeling was that Rayner had brooded on what he thought was his bastardy, his father being so eminent and he himself so poor. Some parties considered that the bitterness from this should lead to a call for mercy. On 28 March, Rayner's defending solicitor received five thousand letters with copies of the petition.

The young man was finally reprieved and subsequently served twelve years of his sentence of life. This was announced in the press on 1 April; *The Times* reported that 'The Home Secretary has advised the King to respite the capital sentence on Horace Rayner with a view to commutation to one of penal servitude for life.' This information went to the man's solicitor, Mr Pierron, and the public had been so involved that the letter, saving the life of their cause celebre, was printed in full:

'Home Office, Whitehall, March 30 1907

Sir, I am directed by the Secretary of State to inform you that he has under his consideration the case of Horace George Rayner, who was sentenced to death at the last sessions of the Central Criminal Court for murder, and in view of all the circumstances he had felt warranted in advising His Majesty to respite the capital sentence, with a view to its commutation to penal servitude for life.

I am Sir, your obedient servant
C. E. Troup, Assistant Under-Secretary.'

What then happened – and this was a ritual that had happened time and again down the centuries – was that the prison governor (in this instance, at Pentonville) went to tell Rayner the good news. It is known what Rayner's response was; he said, *'Thank God for my poor wife's sake. But so far as I am personally concerned I would have preferred to get the whole business over and done with instead of having to endure years of misery behind bars.'*

His solicitor was more grateful, making a special point of telling the media that he thanked all who had assisted him in the campaign for the reprieve.

What strikes us now, looking back at this, is how different the outcome was to the classic template of the McNaghten assassination attempt – the latter being considered insane. With Rayner it was more a case of compassion, and there is no doubt that the attempted suicide was a major factor in the success of the petition. But a plain comparison of the would-be killer who was destined for an asylum for life and this young man, who actually took a life, seems to sway sympathy against Rayner. Something about his fantasy of himself and who he really was touched the imagination of the age in which so many young, middle class men and women were 'finding themselves' in the new expanding world of materialism, self-made business, and massive shifts in the demography of the towns and the commuter class. In some ways, Rayner's act was almost an empathic appeal to all those who felt that same fantasy or dream of being made – of having, as Dickens put it – great expectations.

Whiteley's shop went on until 1981. But one extremely good deed from Whiteley was his million pound bequest for accommodation for 'aged poor persons.' This led to the Whiteley Village Foundation, and the first resident villager was Miss Eliza Palmer, who moved into her new home on 10 October, 1917. Something really good came from the great self-indulgent man who loved his empire and his power; if he had given Rayner money or listened to him for a moment, who knows, he may have lived long enough to play a part in the Great War, but we have to feel that he would have seen that as a massive business opportunity.

16

Appeals Allowed 1907

The year 1907 will forever be resonant with the sound of progress and reform in the legal history of Britain. At last, there was a court of criminal appeal. As discussed in the first chapter, the only appeals in criminal cases before this date were either on a point of law, which was then put before a group of judges at the Crown Cases Reserved Court, or to the superior courts by way of magistrates or other official persons.

But the 1907 Act was truly revolutionary; it gave any person indicted on a criminal offence an unrestricted right of appeal, and it included all cases – whether tried at assizes or in quarter sessions. That meant that both on legal procedure and on new evidence, an appeal could go ahead; it also meant that an appeal could be created on the sentence itself or on the verdict.

There were to be three judges sitting on appeal, and these were High Court judges. The established concept of mercy, lodged in the Home Secretary and the Crown, still remained unchanged; it was the Secretary of State who could refer a case to appeal, as well as other channels of address through solicitors. There had been a recommendation for this as early as 1892, but the opposition was powerful and loud. Sir Henry James had tried to have such a bill passed in 1890, and the essence of that bill was in the text of the 1907 Act.

What this means may easily be understood today by having a cursory look at the books summarising the appeal court records; there, cases from all over the country as well as from the Old Bailey come before the judges and arguments are heard; as we read these, every sentence takes us nearer to a statement that will either, if the case is a capital offence, end in 'sentence confirmed' or 'sentence quashed.' The reprieve of a condemned man would sometimes come after extended discussion. But on the other hand, sometimes it took only a few minutes to confirm a sentence. Of course, many of the cases heard are not for capital offences, but it is not difficult to imagine the sense of drama and expectancy in such a court. The barrister in question, defending the plaintiff, would know that something special was needed.

The great lawyers and advocates were, of course, much in demand in this context. It needs to be recalled that the personality as well as the skills of the advocate were essential in the nineteenth century, when the accused could not speak. Lord Birkett wrote of one of the very best of these men, Edward Marshall Hall, 'Knowing the details of the case as I did, I listened to his every word with a fascinated wonder and amazement. When he came to his peroration and depicted the figure of justice holding the scales until the presumption of innocence was put there to turn the scale in favour of the prisoner, not only was the jury manifestly impressed, but they indeed … were under a kind of spell.'

But there was no jury in the court of appeal; the High Court judges were hard nuts to crack. In the early years of the court, many of the homicide cases before them were murders of wives by husbands or lovers by the supposedly beloved. Consequently, the records of the court make compulsive reading, as every facet of human relationships is there under scrutiny.

There was opposition, of course. Just before this law was passed, there had been the case of Adolf Beck, a Norwegian who had been convicted and given a long prison sentence but whose case turned out to be one of mistaken identity. Naturally, that had an impact on the contemporary debate. Most people realised that a less restricted right of appeal was essential after such suffering by an innocent man. One writer to the newspapers wrote: 'To frame a bill for a less difficult right of appeal would not be hard to do.' But many thought that appeal in any area of law was asking too much, such as a circuit judge who wrote to *The Times*: 'But to give convicted prisoners an unrestricted right of appeal "on the facts" is most violently opposed to the most cherished principles of our laws and to the chief bulwark of our liberties – trial by jury. It is an unconstitutional interference with the protection of the wronged.' In other words, an appeal, such as was suggested, appeared to some to have forgotten the victims.

Many thought that the office of judge was under threat, that he would become a 'legal underling' as one writer said, 'conducting an immediate enquiry to the satisfaction of the prisoner.' But perhaps most open to criticism was the possibility that a killer could escape the noose because of a trivial point of law or a minor error somewhere in the conduct of a trial (as was evident in chapter 4). In effect, one of the most important concerns was that a victim in an assize trial could know that a decision against the accused and even a sentence of death or a long prison term, could be reversed or annulled.

The first assize trials were aware of this, and in October of this year at the Western Circuit assizes, Mr Justice Darling took the opportunity (knowing that the press would report his statements) to express his opinions. He said, 'Certain fears had been expressed that the Act would militate against the accused because, if a conviction took place, the jury knew that an appeal could be lodged … What, in his opinion would be much more likely to take place would be that a judge, or Recorder, or Chairman of Quarter Sessions might decide in favour of the prisoner's request for a case to be reserved, and not in favour of the Crown, who could not ask for a case.' Ideally, only the guilty would be condemned; but everyone knows how miscarriages of justice happen, and always did happen.

At the same time, another judge, Mr Justice Jelf on the Oxford Circuit, made a very important point when he spoke in a similar way to Darling, saying: 'It was much desired that the Court of Criminal Appeal would see its way to weed out at an early stage a very large proportion of the very numerous appeals or applications for leave to appeal which would probably be the first outcome of the Act, and would practically confine the application of its provision to the few case where a real miscarriage could be shown to have taken place.' He was largely correct; there was a process of weeding out. But of course, some cases heard at appeal were there in relation to the old, enduring defences of insanity. In the early courts, if there had been an error it was often related to the problems of defining insane behaviour rather than to serious miscarriages of justice or errors that would lead to an execution.

The very first meeting of the Court of Criminal Appeal took place on 15 May, 1907. *The Times* noted the occasion:

'… there is nothing strictly analogous in civil procedure. The Court of Appeal often sets aside the verdicts of juries on various grounds. But as a rule, the matter of dispute goes to another jury, to be determined by it. Under the new Act, the verdict of a jury may be set aside, and a verdict of not guilty to be decided by the judges. That is enough to show the gravity of the change. We are in the presence of a new system which in the long run may do some good ...'

In other words, to be ironical for a moment, 'the jury was still out' on the virtues of the new Court.

As had been predicted by the professionals, many appeal applications were never successful; but this was the first one heard. It was 'a case which told neither for or against the new Act' according to the *Times* reporter. At the first trial, the judge had not been happy with the verdict, and in the years before this, the matter would probably have gone to Crown Cases Reserved.

In effect, the Act opened up many new potential aspects of a criminal career as well as to advances in the judicial system. Major villains would find themselves having more publicity, for instance. It tended to increase the public persona of the judge, and maybe added more understanding on the part of the public about the many things a judge does in his profession. A prisoner lodging an appeal immediately becomes something other than an obscure forgotten non-person in a cell, outside social norms; the person may have bail and be observed and reported on every time he or she walks into court. But in practical terms, it was the fear of bureaucracy and a paper mountain that deterred the legal professionals in 1907; one reporter said that, 'There is the fact that annually some ten thousand persons are sentenced, and that theoretically each one of them may make use of the machinery of the Act.' As Shakespeare noted, the law meant 'delay', and Dickens's famous case of Jarndice *v.* Jarndice in *Bleak House* reiterates that fact very strongly. It was and still is a slow process.

Today we not only have the same appeal court, we also have the Criminal Cases Review Commission, but as the case of Sean Hodgson shows, as he was released in 2009 after serving a long sentence for a murder he did not commit, however much paperwork is involved, the public must surely feel that 'safety valve' measures for the wrongly convicted should be not only be maintained but financed and expanded.

The Court of Criminal Appeal in 1907 was a wonderful innovation; the newness wore off, and the flood of applications was reduced when it became clear than many failed. But it is easy to underestimate what was actually changed; the most significant aspect of the whole reform is surely the fact that in criminal trials on indictable offences, there was the possibility that a jury's Not Guilty verdict could be reversed.

In the complex history and structure of the courts in English law, there have been a number of circuitous routes towards representations of innocence for those condemned; in the instance of potential insanity, moves towards more liberal attitudes had been made in the 1884 Criminal Lunatics Act, in which it was ruled that where insanity was suspected, two doctors appointed by the Secretary of State would inspect and test the person in question; they would then write a report. So there were steps being taken to try to reduce the number of problems occurring in murder cases where insanity was in focus.

If justice is, as the great Justinian wrote, 'the constant and perpetual wish to render to everyone his due' then the very notion of appeal is essentially a part of the process of justice; after all, juries are notoriously whimsical and capricious. John Mortimer said that 'Juries are like Almighty God: unpredictable.' The 1907 Act was one great step towards having procedures in place to cater for the miscarriages of justice. It is generally felt that the Adolf Beck case, referred to earlier in this chapter, was a formative event in this statute's creation. That does make sense, as Beck was sentenced to several years of penal servitude after the remarkable series of events which led the jury to doubt his claim of mistaken identity. Part of this sensational case was the fact that the testimony of a handwriting expert about Beck's script was a key element in his conviction. When the expert in question was involved in another trial later, the great forensic scientist, Bernard Spilsbury, made use of that weakness, as his biographer notes: '"I find it difficult in this case," he went on, "to get out of my mind this fact, that the name of the handwriting expert who led to the conviction of Adolf Beck was Gurrin – not the present Mr Gurrin …"' In other words, errors by experts were always recalled, and that significance was yet another factor in the argument for an appeal facility.

In the end, this was a momentous event in the history of criminal law. It may have led to drama and controversy, and there may have been teething troubles, but as the twentieth century wore on, to the later Act of 1966 which abolished it and transferred it to the Criminal Division of the Court of Appeal, its chronicles have included cases of espionage, multiple murder and top-level fraud. The volumes of the case records will always provide the more exciting context of the many side-shows of the law.

Edward Lawrence 1909

This is a tragic story of drink, homicide and a trail of wrecked lives, and it ranks as arguably the most sensational criminal case from Wolverhampton. Recently (2009) a book has been devoted to the case by John Benson (see bibliography). It is a story that shows, exceptionally vividly, what the various levels of social history are that gather around a sensational and dramatic crime. It is riddled with class power, exploitation and sheer hasty selfishness. The man at the centre of the tale, Edward Lawrence, had everything that should have led to a comfortable, wealthy and fulfilled provincial life. But none of this was enough for him. In fact, the tragedy at the heart of this horrendous tale is perhaps located within the man himself; his empty, hungry and soulless core of being that led him only to destroy, and never to create.

Edward was born into a rich family; his father, Joseph, moved from Liverpool, where Edward was born in 1867, to Wolverhampton, where his acumen as a public house entrepreneur meant that he became wealthy and powerful. He had started out in life as a pub tenant but did well; in the West Midlands, his empire grew to include seven licensed premises by 1896. Joseph was a heavy drinker and he died in 1901, leaving the huge sum of £49,000. Of course, in terms of social regard, to have become wealthy through trade at that time always meant that there would be some who looked down on you.

Yet the Lawrence family did very well indeed, and in spite of the related habits of bad health and alcoholism linked to those in the hotel and beer shop trade, Joseph was widely respected. He became one of the board members of Wolverhampton Wanderers F.C., and stood for office in local politics. Joseph was elected as a councillor and did that work until 1897. He died in 1901, and left a fine inheritance for his family, although his marriage had failed.

As for Edward, he had an excellent education, first going to the Weston School near Bath, with his younger brother. The institution typified the kind of place where a commercial education, for the new rich of industrialism, could be obtained, the subjects being instilled along with the practical education. Sport was highly prized on the curriculum and Edward would have absorbed many of the values of the Victorian middle class, the codes of honour and behaviour expected of a gentleman. This was followed by a step which comes as something of a surprise to the modern reader; Edward went to train as a veterinary surgeon, studying in Edinburgh. He did well, completing his training in 1887 and becoming a Fellow of the Royal College of Veterinary Surgeons. Although he did not practise when he eventually went home, he kept the subscriptions going and liked having the letters after his name, naturally.

What Edward did do – and it was something unusual for his peers at the time – was travel. There were openings for vets in Argentina, and he went there after setting up in practice in Shifnal, where there was too much established competition. In 1895, there were 21,000 Britons in that country who had been born elsewhere; as John Benson has written: 'Despite the country's climate, it was possible for those living in this part of South America to enjoy some of the trappings of an English, middle-class way of life.'

Edward Lawrence clearly did enjoy this phase of his life and it must have added an edge to his personality – something that would perhaps give him charm, apparent *savoir faire* and maturity when he moved in society back home. He did not stay abroad for long. By 1891 he was home and was in the family business. When Joseph died later, Edward's career meant he was more than ready to take over; he married Margaret Groom (in a registry office). But it is from that time that his dark side emerged.

Edward was a heavy drinker, but he also had a violent streak in him. He must have seemed the happy family man to outsiders; he and Margaret had seven children, and they moved to a roomy and stylish house in the suburbs of the town. What was happening, however, was that Edward was hiring servants and he started his womanising in earnest; he had a mistress, and no doubt met plenty of other women because he travelled to the races and of course, spent time with bar staff, no doubt hiring the attractive young women he fancied in those posts.

Eventually, the 'regular' mistress came on the scene, and she was indeed the *femme fatale* of myth and fiction; Ruth Hadley met Edward in 1904, when he was in charge of the business and very much a part of the social scene around the licensed victualler's profession. Ruth was working class and the daughter of a locksmith. Their affair was soon far from covert; everyone talked and of course, Margaret knew. Edward set up house with the mistress as well as the wife, and in 1904, they were both pregnant with his children.

The sign that Edward was moving out of all restraint came when he was aggressive to Margaret and he attacked her, saying that he would break her jaw. She was seriously injured, and she took him to court. It is not hard to imagine the extent of the local scandal. The case was heard in the police court; a scene that would have been totally demeaning to both, and we have to note that Margaret was a tough and remarkable woman to take matters that far. At first the sentence was for a month's custodial sentence with hard labour, but after consideration, this was revised to a fine of £5 plus costs.

It was the beginning of the end for Edward, in the sense that the downward path to ruin had been set. Edward moved in with his mistress. This was a tempestuous relationship, to say the least. Edward stepped out of the business, and he was paying alimony to Margaret; his drinking became worse. He started his own separate business, called the Midland Brewery, and gave that plenty of time and energy, yet he took another lover called Lottie Davis, and so he was trying to please both Ruth and Lottie as matters became extreme and very worrying. On one occasion, after a row, Ruth took their child and left to stay with a cousin. When she came back, with her cousin as a witness, Edward opened the door with a gun in his hand. It was a foreboding of things to come, a shadow across the lawn of their relationship.

The quarrels between the lovers increased and people knew of it. He was still seeing two other women, and she was costing him money, of course. He had by this time garnered a very bad reputation locally. They were back together at Christmas, 1908, but on the 29 December the worst thing imaginable happened. Edward accused Ruth of being drunk and he ordered her to leave the house; she refused, and this exchange took place:

Edward: 'Now go out of my house ...'
Ruth: 'Give me my week's wages.'
Edward: 'I haven't got any ... Now go out of my house when I tell you.'

Later, they were alone, and the next-door neighbours said in court that they 'heard something go off.' A doctor called Galbraith who lived nearby was posting a letter when Edward rushed out to get his attention. He had shot Ruth Hadley.

Later reports noted that there were no signs of a struggle, and Edward repeatedly said that he had shot in self-defence. She was not yet dead, and Edward was arrested on a charge of attempted murder. There was a revolver on his person; it was looking bleak for him. His statement given at first was that 'I took the revolver out of her hand as soon as she had shot herself, and put it in my pocket ... I knew bloody well she would shoot herself. She only put it to her head like this ... and pulled the thing ...'

Then, after Ruth had died, two police inspectors called on him and he was charged and arrested – 'with having at Wolverhampton on the 29 December 1908 feloniously, wilfully and of malice aforethought ... did kill and murder one Ruth Hadley.' The series of court appearances began; there were the first inquests, and Dr Powell stated that there were three holes – two in the temple and one in the right shoulder. A piece of lead was found in the skull. But on remand, Edward had been quite severely ill; he had had medical attention after being moved to Stafford prison for palpitations, and although he was bruised in various places, the main concern was that he was potentially likely to be deranged, and his alcoholism was known.

The conclusion at the inquest was that the wounds were not self-inflicted and so Edward Lawrence was charged with wilful murder. He was to appear at Stafford assizes in March, 1909. Judge Jelf presided, and the story was told yet again – Edward claiming that there had been a struggle as he tried to disarm the woman, who was unstable. But Edward Lawrence was defended by the great Marshall Hall, and they were going for manslaughter.

The aim was to make Ruth Hadley seem to be a thoroughly awful character with no trace of any reputation that might be considered worthy and respectable. Hall made much of that for the jury's sake. Therefore, Edward pleaded not guilty and it might have seemed an easy task but of course, there had been witnesses to Edward previously carrying a gun. The defence insisted that there was no evidence of suicide, nothing to confirm a fight, and no reason for an act of self-defence. Various servants and bystanders were called; Hall made it clear that the heavy drinking was to be a ploy for the defence – making sure that everyone knew that alcoholism ran through the whole family of victuallers. Hall also took on the prosecution with regard to the revolver and the positions of firing. He was up against solid evidence on ballistics.

But then the turn in Edward's favour came; Marshall Hall exercised his old magic, making sure that his witnesses were going to show that Ruth Hadley was violent and capable of anything with a gun in her hands. When it came to the last phase, on day five, Hall came into his own; being successful most famously in effecting changes of opinion and attitude in juries. He spoke to them before they retired to consider a verdict; he made Edward Lawrence seem a perfect gentleman to have taken back into his home 'a reckless, violent, impossible woman' and to back that up, he made sure that they were aware of the accused man's resolve to win back his family and to conform to the behaviour expected of a family man. Ruth's words: 'He will either kill me or I'll kill him' were said once again for the jury's benefit.

After half an hour, the jury returned and the verdict was not guilty. Edward left the court a free man, with his wife Margaret waiting for him. The locals indulged in plenty of gossip and many thought that he was a very lucky man indeed. As the judge had told him, he 'had had a most terrible lesson.' He died on 8 August, 1912. But even as late in his life as 1910, he was in trouble again; this time a bailiff served him a summons to the county court. His neck might have been saved, but his reputation was not only in tatters; it was shredded and so flimsy that heads would turn and tongues would talk: Edward Lawrence was indeed a local anti-hero. Such was the nature of this extraordinary life that, as his biographer John Benson would surely agree, it reads stranger than fiction.

18

The Tragedy of Mrs Castle:
Driffield 1923

In February, 1923, Mrs Grace Castle put her three children in the bath at her home in Market Place. As if possessed and driven by an inner voice, she forced their heads under the water and drowned them. Three children, the oldest only seven, were found just before midnight that night when police arrived. It has to have been one of the most tragic events in the chronicles of Yorkshire murder. In fact, the very word *murder* is paradoxically unfitting. Poor Grace Castle was in need of help; her mind was deranged and she had allowed a terrible voice of unreason and destruction to creep into her being.

On that horrendous evening, she had tried to ring her husband Fred, who was at a Freemasons' meeting. But there had been no telephone there. Circumstances conspired that evening to lead the woman to kill. Her husband was a good man, and had fought in the Great War, coming home to work as a brewer's manager at Market Place. He had also been a well-known local footballer, playing for Driffield and for Cranswick. Not only did she kill her sons, bit she tried to take her own life as well, taking a tincture of iodine. The poignant situation here was that in her mind she had killed the family 'for him.'

When the police officer arrived, Grace Castle was sitting in the kitchen in a state of mental turmoil, saying, 'Oh Mr Waind, you don't know why I have done it!' Why she had done it is difficult to explain but her own words were, in a piece she wrote in her notebook:

'Whatever happens don't spend a penny on me. I am cursed and so are my children. The only way I was to have saved their souls was to have killed them … Now I cannot see a way out at all. My husband is the best father and a fine man. He worships his children and what a disappointment for him to have seen them grow up in desperation and crime …'

An insight into her condition was provided by the maid in the house, Alice Harper, who was with Mrs Castle earlier that evening. She said that the children were put to bed about a quarter to eight, but that when the children were asleep, Grace was in pain. Alice thought she was suffering from her usual neuralgia. But everyone managed to get to bed, and Alice was roused from her sleep at eleven thirty and she saw Grace sitting in the kitchen saying that her head felt funny and then she said, 'Oh my poor bairns!'

At the first meeting of the coroner's inquest, it was a brief affair and was adjourned. Thomas Holtby, the coroner, summed up the feeling at the time when he said that the deaths constituted the 'saddest tragedy' he had come across. The inquest was adjourned until there was medical evidence. The Rev. George Storer presided at the funeral of the children. Grace Castle was charged with murder, having malice aforethought, and of course, was guilty of attempted suicide as well.

Above: The Caledonian Asylum.

Right: Page from Insanity Report.

COMMITTEE ON INSANITY AND CRIME,

REPORT

OF THE

Committee appointed to consider what changes, if any, are desirable in the existing law, practice and procedure relating to criminal trials in which the plea of insanity as a defence is raised, and whether any and, if so, what changes should be made in the existing law and practice in respect of cases falling within the provisions of section 2 (4) of the Criminal Lunatics Act, 1884,

Presented to Parliament by Command of His Majesty.

LONDON:
PRINTED & PUBLISHED BY HIS MAJESTY'S STATIONERY OFFICE.
To be purchased directly from H.M. STATIONERY OFFICE at the following addresses:
Imperial House, Kingsway, London, W.C.2; 28, Abingdon Street, London, S.W.1;
York Street, Manchester; 1, St. Andrew's Crescent, Cardiff;
or 120, George Street, Edinburgh;
or through any Bookseller.

1924

Price 6d. net.

Then, at the resumed inquest, some medical evidence came from the family doctor, Dr Keith, a man who had fought alongside Fred Castle in the war. He confirmed that Grace had suffered from some kind of nervous condition for six months; Keith had attended on the night of the deaths and there he found that she had presumably taken the iodine simply because it was something 'chemical', as it was hardly the type of substance a person would take if they wanted to die quickly. All she could say was that the doctor would see by her writings why she had done it. She was totally distracted and, although aware of what she had done and how she had killed, it was all somehow unreal to her, and outside her range of comprehension.

She was detained in Hull gaol awaiting her trial, and at this point the journalists had begun to be annoyingly insensitive and intrusive, so much so that a member of the jury requested that he make a statement on this, saying that he wished to express strong disapproval of the flash-lights and cameras being used. Through modern eyes, there is nothing unusual or unexpected in this, but in 1923, the moral universe was more rigid and especially in the quieter areas in the provinces, a 'big story' in the eyes of a journalist out to make a name for himself was far from that – it was a terrible local sadness.

At York Assizes in March, Dr Howlett, the prison doctor in Hull, was called to give an assessment of Grace's condition. He confirmed what Dr Simpson, the Medical Superintendent of the East Riding, had said, that though she could put into words the sequence of events on that tragic night, she was unable to feel any impression of emotion or meaning from this. Consequently both medical men agreed that she was insane. In fact, Simpson noted that it was a case of 'long-standing insanity.'

Her youngest son, Kenneth, had been only three, and it was noted during the investigation that Grace Castle had been 'in a poor state of health' since Kenneth's birth. As clues to why she chose to kill in this way and for the reasons given, we can theorise that partly her reasons were altruistic – thinking that the one she loved would be better for the lack of stress caused by worry about the children, and also that her own problems (depression) would be alleviated. The tincture of opium is an interesting detail, because it bears no relation to any substance used commonly in these contexts; using that has the hallmark of desperation and irrational thought. It also seems highly likely that Grace Castle was suffering from post-natal depression, and in the circumstances in which she had to live, little was done to address this. The spirit of the times was to press on regardless. Even with a maid and help around the house, Grace was still under pressure, and it was from a deep well of unhappiness within her.

Grace Castle was therefore unfit to plead and was admitted to Broadmoor on 9 March, 1923. The historian Helen Stewart has tried to follow up the future course of the parents' lives but little has emerged. A man who went to the funeral of the children recalled that Fred Castle had been ill in later life, and had remained a Freemason, but as to Grace, we know nothing of her later life and her ultimate fate stays a mystery.

In Driffield cemetery the gravestone can still be seen, giving testimony to one of the most melancholy stories ever told about murders within a family. There it is recorded that Donald, Hubert and Kenneth Castle rest in peace and that their deaths were 'in tragic circumstances.'

19

The Wallace Enigma 1931

If Liverpool can claim to be the setting for several infamous and problematic homicides, then first among these has to be the Wallace case. 1931 was a notable year for crime mysteries. There was the notorious 'Blazing Car' case in Northumberland, still unsolved, and also the Margaret Schofield case in Dewsbury (unsolved). But in sheer complexity, the death that has been called by many 'the perfect murder' is Liverpool's own, and presents the historian with a riddle: if William Wallace, gentle chess-playing insurance agent living in a quiet suburb, did indeed create an alibi and a hoax, then why did he make it all so difficult for himself? There were easier ways to create a ruse and a suspicious stranger.

The story began on 19 January, 1931, when a phone call was made to the Central Chess Club in Liverpool by a man calling himself Qualtrough. He wanted to see Wallace urgently, on a business matter. Wallace was not yet at his club, but he was due to arrive to play a match at seven o'clock. Wallace arrived at twenty to eight, and then he was told about the phone call. The club was at the City café, and Wallace had not been doing too well of late, walking the streets for the Prudential. This call meant a potential customer, so he asked about the address given. Here lies the heart of the mystery; Qualtrough said he lived at Menlove Gardens East – an address that did not exist. Wallace asked several people about the address, and it was known that there was a street called Menlove Gardens North.

All this became important when Wallace's steps are traced the next day, when he went in search of the mystery man. He left his home in Wolverton Street and went to Smithdown Road; then he caught a number 4 tram at Lodge Lane. We know that he went to Menlove Gardens and started looking for 'East' in the area. He made a point of asking lots of people about the address. But by eight he had given up and went home. It was when he arrived home, just before nine, that he found the body of his wife. Julia Wallace lay in a pool of her own blood, in her cosy room.

The Wallaces were a quiet couple; neighbours reported no scenes of anger or disagreement. William was a bookish man; he read Marcus Aurelius and based his behaviour and attitudes on that Roman's stoical philosophy. He was firm and controlled right through the coming investigation and trial; this was something that was surely against him. The image he gave was of a callous, unfeeling man, who should have shown extreme emotion after the violent killing of his wife in their own home. Wallace had been born in the Lake District in 1878; he had worked for a short while in India, and then in Ripon, before settling down to the life of a clerk in Liverpool. He had married Julia in 1913.

The scene of the crime was horrific. When Wallace came home, he could not open the front door, so he went around to the back. He managed to enter, walked upstairs, and found nothing unusual; but when he went down to the parlour and turned on the

Photo, Vandyk.

Lawyer, Mr Justice Humphries.

Mrs Wallace.

Mr Wallace.

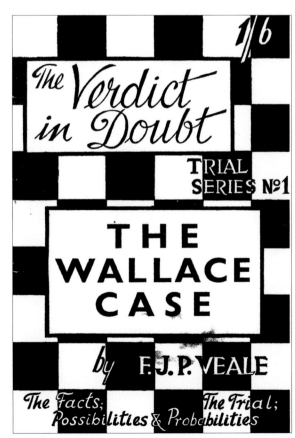

An early study of the Wallace case.

light, there was her body, lying face down on the rug. There was a pool of blood around her head and such was the force of a blow to her head that bone was visible. Wallace was accompanied by a friend, Jack Johnson, as he saw this, and Johnson went to bring a police officer. Meanwhile Wallace realised that his insurance takings had been stolen from a box in the kitchen. But it was puzzling that a jar of pound notes in the bedroom had not been taken, despite the fact that they were smudged with blood.

When PC Williams arrived, he and Wallace checked details, but then the forensic expert came: Professor MacFall. He discovered no less than ten more wound marks on the head. There was a mess in the house – evidence of an apparent frenzy. But MacFall noted that the gas-lights were out, so the rage and the supposed search for booty would have taken place in the dark. Also, there were no blood-marks in places where one would have expected them, such as on door-handles for instance.

Clearly, Wallace himself would have to be questioned intensively, as there were so many pointers to an alibi and so many oddities at the scene of the murder that did not seem to square with the supposed crazed murder and attack. DS Hubert Moore led the investigation. He had long experience; over thirty years of police work. At Dale Street police station, the interviews began. Attention was paid to the Qualtrough call, and to the witnesses who recalled talking to Wallace on his hopeless quest for Menlove Gardens East. It all appeared to be so fabricated, after all: a phone call at a point when there would be an alibi and yet enough time for Wallace to have made the call himself before arriving at the chess club; then all that asking for directions even to the point of making sure that conversations were memorable. It must have all seemed so purposeful to Moore as he faced this quiet, restrained and inscrutable man who controlled his emotions with perfection.

Amazingly, the Qualtrough phone call was traced; it was made from a box defined as Anfield 1627 – a box only four hundred yards from Wallace's house in Wolverton Street. But evidence at the scene was unavailable: there was no weapon, no prints and no items found even in the drains and sewers. It was noted, though, that a poker was missing. More important, what would be the motive? Julia had only twenty pounds due from insurance on her life. Wallace had no need for that; he had money saved in his account. At the trial, people started looking for motives in the area of personality and relationship, even to noting Wallace's diary entries, such as one comment about Julia's 'aimless chatter.' But in context, he had written this after her death, saying that he missed her 'loving smiles and aimless chatter.'

The trial began on 22 April at St George's hall. The judge was Mr Justice Wright; for the prosecution there was E. G. Hemmerde, and Roland Oliver for the defence. They were all brilliant lawyers in their way, but they were to find several anomalies and unanswered questions in this affair. Wallace's own statement included his own assertion that any hint of him having killed his wife was 'monstrous.' In gathering evidence for the defence, they had to concentrate on the timing of a milk delivery at the murder house; a certain Elsie Wright, who was sure that the call at the house, at which Julia was alive, was close to a quarter to seven, not half past six. Little details such as this would count for a great deal in the case, as everything rested on the movements of Wallace around Liverpool that day.

Everything except the issue of the raincoat; Wallace's mackintosh was under Julia's body. Here, the limitations of forensics at the time were exposed, particularly in blood movements and splattering; the blood on this coat being either caused by the wounding, or in fact dripping after death. There were also burn stains on the coat, so another question arose: did Wallace fail in an attempt to burn the material? Or equally sensible was the line of thought that it could have been burned in the attack, because Julia was close to the gas fire.

The questioning by the prosecution was aimed at locating all the strange and oddly convenient circumstances of the phone call, the attempt to find the address, and the arguably transparent and feeble creation of an alibi. It had also seemed unconvincing that an innocent man would have walked upstairs in his home before going through to the parlour; the implication being that he was fabricating a likely 'geography' of the movements of the supposed frenzied attacker. Equally, in the examination of Julia Wallace's nature and character, it had been made extremely unlikely that she would have a lover, so if the motive of the anonymous killer was related to a crime of passion, then where was the evidence for that? In the early afternoon of the fourth day of the trial, the jury retired to consider their verdict. Their decision was that Wallace was guilty of wilful murder. The judge stated that it was a 'murder unexampled in the annals of crime.'

After the death sentence was passed, Wallace still showed no response. *The Liverpool Post and Echo* reported that 'Wallace's bearing after the verdict was as calm and impassive as throughout the trial, and when asked if he had anything to say, he replied in a quiet tone, "I am not guilty. I don't want to say anything else."'

But that is not the end of the story. At the Court of Appeal on 19 May, 1931, his case was reconsidered; this was after he was moved to Pentonville in April, and after prayers were being said for him in Liverpool Cathedral. He played the violin, and as death was looming, his violin and his chess set had been brought to him. In Pentonville, though, he was housed in the death cell.

Hemmerde took a long time at appeal to elaborate on how all the evidence stacked against his client was circumstantial. There was a forty-five minute wait for Wallace, before he would know if he were to hang or not. Lord Hewart had found three clear elements which had to be weighed and discussed: first, Mr Oliver had not said that there was no case to answer in the original trial; secondly, was the summing up done with accuracy? Third, as Hewart said, 'The whole of the evidence was closely and critically examined … The court was not concerned with suspicion, however grave, or with theories, however ingenious.' In using section four of the 1907 Criminal Appeal Act, Hewart quashed the conviction.

The last word has to go to Wallace himself. He said, 'I hardly knew what it all meant. It seemed ages before he reached the sentence which conveyed to me the knowledge to step out of the dock, free.'

But the stigma is such an affair does not go away; by the end of 1932, he had moved away from Anfield and he was a sick man, with kidney disease. He died in Clatterbridge Hospital on 26 February 1933; he was buried with his wife in Anfield cemetery.

20

Jeannie Donald 1934

This has to be the classic template case of lingering doubt, theory and supposition. It has the added dimension of interest we find in stories embedded in the ordinary, and in which the suspicious death at the heart of the enigma was never satisfactorily explained by forensic enquiry. The murder of Helen Priestly, eight and a half years old, in April, 1934, in Urquhart Road, Aberdeen, appears to be resigned to the 'unsolved' category, in spite of the best minds in criminal analysis being applied to the known facts. Even the great William Roughead, doyen of true crime writers, admitted that all was left, after the facts were given and the evidence assessed, was a puzzle, albeit one that offered a temptation for commentators and criminologists to apply their own thoughts.

Helen's body was found after a night's searching in the lobby of her parent's home in the tenements, and she was in a sack, with her feet projecting out; the sack had not been in the lobby at two in the morning of that day, and it was first discovered around five, after hope had almost gone that the girl would be found. She had been sexually interfered with, and there had been a reported cry of 'She's been used!' from someone during the chaos of the discovery and the gathering crowd that wanted to be present at the gruesome scene.

The story begins with Helen being sent out by her mother to buy a loaf of bread. She did not return and a search began. Jeannie Donald lived with her husband and daughter in the flat below the Priestly family. The neighbours searched around the street for hours, and Jeannie later said that she had been out at a local pavilion fair with her daughter, all evening until eleven p.m. In spite of the apparent alibi of all members – Mr Donald being at work that day as a hairdresser – Jeannie was arrested and charged.

There was a police operation, and the green area behind the tenement was inspected for footprints; then of course, the body and the sack were studied. Several famous scientists were involved in that work, including the charismatic Professor Sydney Smith. All the medical men found several details of great interest. There were cinders in the sack and in the child's mouth and hair. There were some small traces of blood there too. The cause of death was asphyxia, but there was an interesting fact here: Helen had an enlarged thymus and any pressure on that would have easily caused death.

There were signs of apparent rape, but on closer inspection, a perforation of the lower bowel and other signs of injury by a smallish and thin object. Professor Glaister from Glasgow University was a specialist in hair analysis and he looked at hairs found in the sack, in the Donald hearth, and in a brush taken from Jeannie Donald while on remand. All the expert could say was that there was a striking similarity; he had no definite confidence in saying they were all from the same source: Helen Priestly. At the trial, as William Roughead wrote: 'A long and learned cross-examination by Mr Blades left the matter much where it was.'

But some work of much more significance came from the evidence given by Professor Mackie of Edinburgh who explained that a rare bacillus, coli form in nature, was present in the underwear of the dead girl and also in a cleaning cloth in the Donald household.

He said in court: 'I have given this very careful consideration and it is my considered opinion that the findings I have stated are very suggestive that these cloths had been contaminated from the same source as bloodstains on the child's combinations.' He said he would recommend a 'public authority' when faced with this contrast, to take action, and if it were a disease, he would 'recommend action with equal confidence.' Fibres were also examined, by an expert from Bradford, and some found in the sack matched those in the Donald house; but the problem with that was that the Donalds kept lots of sacks for cinders and other waste, and so such materials would be expected.

Far more useful were the findings of Sydney Smith, who was described by Roughead (who was at the trial) in this way: 'An ideal witness, alert but calm, positive but polite, clear, competent and urbane under the most rigorous cross-examination.' He had been the first to spot the coli form bacillus and he examined a large number of items from the Donald house; he looked at fibres and cinders and found matches. The wiping cloth had traces of vomit on it, and that was important later. Smith was also sure that the knickers were torn before there was bleeding, and that the child had at first been lying face-down. What all experts agreed on was that there had been no male rape.

This point was important because that had been taken as a strong possibility. A little boy told police that he had seen Helen being abducted by a man; but later he confessed that he had made up the tale. There was also the reported statement about a man hanging around the area. But several people, who had been involved in the hunt for the girl, later said that there had been no unusual sightings of unknown people as they looked around the whole area in the early hours of the morning.

The crucially vital details that pointed the finger of guilt at Jeannie Donald were that the light on her flat had been seen on at around three in the morning but no-one from her family had come out to help; the sack from her flat, containing the body, had apparently been placed there later in the morning after the main search; there was no evidence of any other person present who could have done the killing; Jeannie Donald and Mrs Priestley, though they had no open confrontations nor anger expressed, did not speak to each other. Jeannie expressed the situation with these words: 'It was because of water coming down; we had no row, only we did not speak ...' All this was fairly strong material to work with. Add to that the established fact that little Helen used to tease and annoy Jeannie in various ways, and the minutiae of the forensic evidence – such as the cinders on the body and in the sack and the mysterious disappearance of a box of ash from the floor in the Donalds' room, and things looked bleak for the accused.

If she were guilty, then it seemed that the body of the little girl must have been kept in the Donald's flat somewhere for several hours – certainly from eleven thirty through to around five a.m. That implied a callous and evil nature behind the reserved and quiet front that Mrs Donald put on for the world when questioned. When the accused was asked why there was no demonstrable involvement from her in the search for the girl and other matters pertaining to Helen, she replied that she had given a shilling towards a wreath. When, in the early hours when the body had been found, a neighbour had said to Jeannie that 'They are thinking that she met her death here ... it was some person about the door ...' Jeannie had said nothing, but simply gone inside her own rooms.

Before leaving for the pavilion with her daughter, Jeannie said that, in the afternoon, two suspicious and disreputable men had called at her house. One she said was a dirty, unshaven old man with his hands in his pockets. It all seems rather weak and stereotyped.

But on the final day of the trial there was a new witness, and the defence counsel, Mr Blades, said that half past three on the afternoon of the killing, a teenager had seen what she thought was a tramp walking with a little girl who had a blue dress, a tammy hat and black stockings. She was also carrying a parcel suggestive of a loaf and she seemed 'scared like.' But this had been already looked into earlier, and there was a suspicion of yet another fabrication.

When the court process was complete, matters were looking bad for Mrs Donald. There were no other suspects and no other related lines of thought. Some things he could use were actions such as a police surgeon who had said that blood was found in the Donald flat but he later changed his mind, and also that the forensics had not been conclusive. The alibi for the afternoon – that Mrs Donald and her daughter had been to the pavilion and had also been shopping at a market – was not contested and no witnesses were called to say yes or no to that claim.

But in the end, as the Lord Advocate reminded everyone in his summing-up, the evidence from Professors Mackie and Smith about the bacillus was hard to deny. There was also the strange business of the Donald's light being on at three in the morning and their absence from the search. The latter point must have been a formative detail in the general condemnation of the accused. It took less than twenty minutes for the jury to reach a decision. There are fifteen people in a Scottish jury and in this case, thirteen found Mrs Donald guilty of murder and two decided it was not proven.

The death sentence was stated; Mrs Donald would 'be hanged in the prison of Aberdeen on 13 August …' But there was an appeal for clemency and for the sentence to be commuted to prison for life. This was done by means of 1926 legislation; The Criminal Appeal (Scotland) Act. This laid down that an appeal had to be lodged within ten days of the sentence, and so the lawyers lost no time, and when the response came from the Scottish office in London it was favourable for the condemned:

'With reference to the case of Jeannie Ewen or Donald, now lying under sentence of death in His Majesty's Prison, Aberdeen, I have to inform you that, after full consideration, I have felt justified in advising His majesty to respite the execution of the capital sentence, with a view to its commutation to penal servitude for life.'

The life was spared but the mystery remains. It is hard not to agree with William Roughead, who sees the solution as being a case of anger on the part of Jeannie Donald, after being once again teased by the girl who called her 'Cocoanut' and banged on her door. Was it just a temper that went too far and a shaking at the neck did damage to the girl with the enlarged thymus gland? Everything after that would be explained by a need to cover up the actual accidental death with signs of attack and rape.

It was in the end, perhaps, a tale of the last straw in a long line of childish torments. Then, all the actions (or lack of action) by the women in the flat downstairs could be interpreted as the hard, disgusting deeds of a killer rather than as the silence of a terrified criminal who knew that she had done something seriously wrong and that the world must not know the truth. It doesn't know the truth today, but the theory of accidental death, on a fragile little girl, makes sense.

With regard to the general view of execution on women, this reprieve was not unusual; there had been others as attitudes changed, but only six months after this case, Ethel Major was hanged in Hull prison for poisoning her husband in the little Lincolnshire village of Kirby on Bain. Britain was not such a civilised country after all, thought many, on that Christmas when the death was reported in the press. Naturally, in Aberdeen, there were many who had no problem with hangings, and they were sorely disappointed that Mrs Donald did not swing on the gallows for killing 'one of their own.'

21

The Mills Case and the Eliza Ray Murder
1934-5

Yet another case of child-murder kept the courts busy the year after Jeannie Donald; this time the focus was in Blackburn. The story concerned a couple in their sixties, Henry and Edith Mills, who lived in John Bright Street, Blackburn, and whose home was something of a playground for local children. In working class communities at that time, and indeed long after, households of older couples were quite often centres of child-minding at all times of the day. In this case, it is clear that a number of small children, and their parents, would gather at the Mills' for tea and chat. But in July, 1935, there was indeed a black cloud hanging over the Mills' place.

A three-year-old girl, Helen Chester, was found dead, with her body severely burned, wrapped in a parcel in the yard of a Mr Farnworth, next door to the Mills' house; the Chesters lived on the other side of the Mills home. The little body was in newspaper and bed linen, tied around with string; there were no legs and the burning was very extreme. But the cause of death had not been burning – the skull had been smashed with a hammer, forensic officers later confirmed.

Helen, when she left her home earlier that day, had been wearing a blazer with metal buttons and a metal chain, which was found in the toilet in the yard outside the Mills' house, with the buttons. Every home had a range then, with a central fire, and after the search for the child and the discovery of the corpse, police made a detailed search of the area, finding in the fire ash some severely charred bones and chunks of fat. Other evidence of grisly death were found elsewhere in the home, with blood stains on the bed and body parts stuffed up waste pipes and down sinks. The medical experts called at the hearing at Blackburn Police court said that bone located in the bedroom matched the thigh of the torso in the parcel. Even the string around the little body matched similar material in the Mills' yard. If this were murder – and indeed it was – then there had been very little attempt to hide evidence at all. What efforts had been made were crass and futile.

Further searches recovered bits of bed quilt from the top of a wall, and so every detail of material located fitted the nature of the remains. Being questioned about all this, Henry Mills said, 'Bones? Oh yes, we had a breast of mutton yesterday, and I threw the bones on the fire.' His equally unintelligent answers to the point that the bones were human were that he had eaten fish. But eventually, when asked the reason why newspaper was bloodstained, he simply replied, 'You have me beat.' When the husband and wife were then charged with murder, Henry said merely, 'Don't say a word' to his accomplice.

Why did this happen? That was the basic question in court, and E. G. Robey, for the Crown, said that it was a mystery, but that it was surely impossible for another person to bring other bones into that house; in other words, the evidence against the couple may have been circumstantial, but it was convincing. The famous old judge Henry

Hawkins favoured circumstantial evidence and openly said so, but in the 1930s there was a little more debate.

At Lancaster Assizes on 17 October the only significant additional data concerned the movements of Henry Mills. He had been across town and had an alibi until after eight in the evening. He said that he heard a councillor making a speech around a quarter to eight as he passed through the market square, and that was verified. As he neared home he saw a neighbour, Mr Pickering, calling for his daughter Margaret, another child who played at the Mills' home. In fact, Mrs Pickering had been sitting with Edith Mills while Henry was away and had not sensed the presence of little Helen. The deceased was last seen at around twenty to eight that evening, playing close to the Mills' house. Given all the material evidence and the lack of any other person in the picture, the couple were sentenced to hang at the Lancaster Assizes, by Mr Justice Hilbery. It was clear at the time in Lancaster that for whatever reason, there had been an intentional act, using a coal hammer, by a person at the Mills' house, and that the attempt at cremation of the body had been a feeble attempt to hide evidence. The defence had concluded on that occasion:

'... that if only one was concerned, the evidence for the Crown left it in doubt which was the guilty party, and that therefore, there being a reasonable doubt whether the one or the other had committed the crime, the case ought to be withdrawn from the jury and a verdict of acquittal entered.'

This was not accepted, and joint guilt was taken, the death sentence following for both.

But there was an appeal. This was based on the ground that Henry's defence had not been adequately put to the jury at Lancaster; also there was the complication of the joint charge and sentence. The appeal was before Justices MacNaghten, Goddard and Atkinson in November, 1935. For Edith Mills, the appeal was that she was profoundly deaf, and so may not have been aware of a murder going on, and may only have been an abettor later on. In any case, as Mr Blackledge said on her behalf, there was no conclusive proof about which of the pair had actually taken the life of the little girl. The jury at Lancaster had recommended mercy for Edith, so there was some reason for thinking that she was seen as the less culpable of the two.

However, there were differentiated opinions in the resulting thinking at appeal; certainly there was doubt about the time that Henry had been present on the day of the death, whereas Edith had been there all the time, and the killing had most likely taken place before he arrived home (as Mrs Pickering was not aware of a living child in the house during her stay of one hour and a quarter). Judge MacNaghten said that in the opinion of the court the conviction of Henry Mills must be quashed, but that the conviction of Edith had to stand.

There was no certainty about Henry Mills' location at the time of the murder; that was established. Then the appeal court made it clear that the view of Edith as the killer in the house was tenable: the conclusion was, as in the record of the court: 'So far as the female appellant is concerned, we think that the learned Judge was right in rejecting the submission made to him at the close of the evidence for the prosecution. There was, in our opinion, ample evidence against her and we see no ground for interfering with the conviction in her case.'

This seems not only harsh, but illogical. The inference that Edith actually committed the act is based on the assumption that the child was killed before Henry arrived, and that had that not been so, the visitor would have know the child was there and alive: this does not follow, as the child may have been playing outside at that time, or playing with older children in another room.

But Edith did escape the noose. On 28 November, her reprieve was announced.

The Eliza Ray murder was equally complex with regard to multiple convictions and appeals. The Lord Chief Justice, Lord Hewart, had an eventful year in 1934: first he had the hugely enjoyable experience of dealing with the humorist A. P. Herbert's playful defence of the right for liquor to be sold in the House of Commons; at the end of the year, he fell in love, when he met the woman who was to be his second wife, New Zealander Jean Stewart. But in between these two uplifting and pleasurable experiences, Hewart had to hear an appeal from three convicted murderers at the Old Bailey.

The case, which became known as the Croyden Murder, concerned three men who had set out to rob the home of Eliza Ray, a widow of seventy-six who lived at 47 Handcroft Road, Croydon. But in that robbery, the woman was killed. An army pensioner called Pennefather lived with her and he went for a long walk every evening between seven-thirty and eight-thirty. When he returned on the evening of 17 February, 1943, he found the landlady dead on the floor. The pensioner used to walk, then stop and have a chat; on one occasion he must have talked to someone about Mrs Ray, and very likely he mentioned that she earned around £12 a month from the rent, and that she kept £3,000 in the house. That is a decidedly crass and stupid thing to talk about, and it is certain that the man he told, called Schulman, then told a criminal called Knowles.

Before long there were three desperate men out to get the old lady's money. They were called Leonard Martin, Albert Ansell and Walter Ross, and they met to plan the job. Only just over a hundred yards from Mrs Ray's house there was a pub called The Derby Arms, and the villains met there. When Pennefather went for his walk, they struck. According to Martin, he said that because he was known in that area, the other two went in the house while he kept watch outside. But when the body was found, she had been gagged with what was later discovered to be Martin's handkerchief. There had been no forced entry and the woman's purse was on a table with only a few coppers in it. Nothing was found and taken; later, Martin was heard to say to Knowles, 'We have turned that rat over and we never found anything … all I left behind me was a handkerchief.'

At the Old Bailey, the three were sentenced to death. But there was a technicality – the judge had made an error with regard to corroboration. Corroboration was needed for evidence from Martin, and in fact the judge stated that there had been corroboration. But he was wrong. At appeal, Mr Manly, speaking for Ansell and Ross, said: 'The most serious ground of complaint is that the judge directed the jury that a conversation alleged to have taken place between Martin and Knowles after the commission of the crime, might be corroboration of Martin's evidence. Such a conversation was not evidence against Ansell and Ross at all.'

At the time, the jury had not picked this up; the verdict was reached with that assumption made. Lord Hewart's logical and precise mind summed up well, explaining at appeal the actions of the three participants on the evening of the murder. Hewart said: '*Now to deal first with Martin. The uncontradicted evidence of Sir Bernard Spilsbury was that the cause of Mrs Ray's death was shock due to asphyxiation … Spilsbury described the injuries which she had received, he said a considerable amount of violence had been used. He said there were several blows … a murder had been committed, but … by whom?*'

He concluded that evidence pointed to the presence of Martin when the killing was done. The fateful words were spoken: 'In our opinion there is no ground at all so far as the appellant Martin is concerned to interfere with his conviction …' He was to hang.

But Ansell and Ross had something else at appeal, as well as the misdirection of the jury at the trial: evidence from a Mr and Mrs Spencer had been omitted at the trial, and their statements were in favour of Ansell and Ross. Their convictions were quashed. They would live.

But there was a petition led by Martin's wife and she went, along with twelve young brothers and sisters, around the Croydon area to gather signatures. The petition was given to the Home Secretary on May 29, and two days later Martin was reprieved. Mrs Martin went with a second batch of signatures and was told, when she said she had more to present, 'You need not bother …'

22

William Edwards 1936

Without the writings of a woman whose life's work is now almost totally forgotten, this story would not be known. This tireless campaigner for the abolition of hanging wrote about this story: *'His case stands out in my memory, amongst those sad cases I can never forget.'* She chose his case for special discussion in her autobiography, a work perhaps most interesting for the photographs of the lady's very large car parked in front of the prisons across the land in the 1930s.

On 26 November, 1936, William Edwards took the life of the woman he loved. Minutes before her death, she had been weeping for fear of losing him, so much did she love him too. Why Violet van der Elst found this story a sad case is that the young man had no idea what he had done. He was an epileptic.

Edwards was twenty-six at the time, a man who had been drifting from job to job since leaving school. He had worked at Tankards Mill in Laisterdyke, Turners, the metal polishers, and as a labourer for Sanda Metal Co. He had been working as a baker's assistant at Newboulds Ltd up to seven weeks before he took Myrtle Parker out for the night. He had met the girl for six months and they had been walking out regularly; he was always at her parents' house in Bierley.

Myrtle was just twenty and worked as a wool spinner; they had met at the Picturedrome in Wakefield Road. They discussed the possibility of getting married in May and she had agreed to marry him. At that time, she was legally a minor (under twenty-one) so Edwards had to obtain a form of consent from the Marriage Registry Office. He had talked about this with Myrtle's mother and she suggested that they wait a while. Matters seem to have been good between them; there was no evidence of any acrimony.

On the fatal night the couple walked for about forty minutes and then he left, but they met again at seven that night and after spending some time at her home, they went out and stopped at Merrydale Road. It was there that, as they talked about their future, Myrtle began to weep and as he later said, 'begged me to stay with her.' This upset Edwards and tipped him over into an epileptic fit. He took out his pen-knife and opened it. The report from the trial has this summary of what happened next:

'His depression deepened and, as now appears from the reconstruction, he took up the knife and whirled his arm, not knowing where the blow fell. His memory failed him. He has no recollection of what else happened.'

Edwards did that with the knife and then wandered the streets until he arrived at a friend's house and there he slept; that was five in the morning. But in the morning he said to his friend, 'I have done my woman in.'

Throughout the nineteenth century there was a continuing debate on what elements of mental illness constituted a defence of insanity and diminished responsibility. In the formative Lincolnshire case of William Drant in the 1870s, the psychologist Maudsley entered the debate and the man who had killed a village constable and had a death sentence was reprieved, as his epilepsy was shown to be the cause of his murderous actions, as explained in chapter 12.

In Edward's case, he was sentenced to death, in spite of evidence from all kinds of sources. First, his friend, Mr Marshall, who had seen him arrive early that morning and had seen his pitiable condition; then two medical men insisted that Edwards' case fulfilled the criteria of epilepsy; frequent headaches, moodiness and groundless loss of temper and a history of many such attacks. Of course, there was also no motive at all; he had taken the life of the women he loved and whom he wished to marry.

In court, the jury heard that four years earlier Edwards had wounded another young lady he was courting. He had stabbed her in the arm with his knife, and for that he was given six month's hard labour. At that previous trial, epilepsy had been argued but had been ineffective. Again, when his life depended on the verdict, Edwards was let down and the judge placed the black cap on his head to pass sentence of death.

Other witnesses had spoken, such as a Mr Ogden, who said that Edwards had lived with him for a few years and that 'He used to sit in the house with his head in his hands. If asked to move, he would become bad-tempered, get up and bang things about … he would for no reason at all, suddenly get up and bang things about … If asked what was the matter he would make no reply.'

The police surgeon, Dr Rimmer, said that his reading of the homicidal incident was that the man had suffered an epileptic fit. But one witness gave a clear account of a seizure:

'About a year ago I was out with Edwards in a public house. He was quite sober. Suddenly, and without reason, he threw a mug of beer at a man who had just walked past him. I hit Edwards on the side of the jaw. It was not a severe blow, but he turned pale and fell to the ground unconscious. He threw his legs and arms about and it was obvious he was in a fit. Two or three days later I spoke to him about it and he had no recollection of the incident.'

Hitting your friend on the jaw to help is a strange way to show concern, but at least it produced the kind of evidence that Edwards' counsel must have been looking for. However, it was all to no avail.

Even Myrtle's father, at the North Bierley Labour Club, saw Edwards in a fit and helped to carry him out. He and another man left him in the rain, thinking that would revive him. But the strongest statement came from Edwards' mother, Amy Edwards, who said that he had had two fits when he was just four years old and that he was three years old before he could talk. She said that as he grew older he would have frightening mood-swings and that he tended to fly into a rage if he was disturbed. He had left home in 1934 and lived with his sister, Mrs Ogden, in Lilac Grove Street.

But the most considerable medical statement came from Dr Frederick Eurich of Edinburgh University and consulting physician at Bradford Royal Infirmary. He said at the trial: 'I have spent three and a half years in a large asylum controlling 2,000 patients, made a special study of mental diseases in England and in Germany … From the facts put before me, I have arrived at the following conclusion, namely that it is highly probable that Edwards suffers from occasional attacks of epilepsy …'

Eurich explained that people like Edwards suffer from loss of memory and waves of depression; he also added that in these states, the depression was likely to lead to periodic fits of violence. Apparently, Edwards lifted Myrtle over a wall after the attack but recalled nothing of that the next day. There had been complete normality earlier on the day of the homicide; Edwards had been at the home of Myrtle's sister, Gladys, and they had both walked to a draper's shop in Tong Street, where Edwards paid for some gloves he had ordered.

Edwards' last statement in court was that for as long as he could remember, he had never felt 'normal in health.' He also stressed that he drank very little alcohol, so that was never a factor in the violence. He was condemned to death, but that was overturned later by the Home Secretary. The campaigner for the abolition of capital punishment, Mrs van der Elst, wrote in her account of the case: 'I hope Edwards will be given plenty of work to do to keep his mind occupied, so that he can work out his own salvation.' She was one of the unsung heroes of the campaign against hanging, parking her large black car at the gates of prisons on execution day and making a nuisance of herself. Mrs van der Elst has given us the fullest account of the Edwards case, and her treatment of the facts was exemplary.

Not all killers in the throes of epilepsy were so fortunate. Also in Bradford, in 1934, Louis Hamilton killed his wife at Stott Hill and he was to claim an attack of *petit mal*, the less severe form of epilepsy. That did not save him from the gallows, and he had an appointment with executioner Thomas Pierrepoint in Armley.

23

Rowland and Simcox:
Three Reprieves and a Hanging

In March, 1964, there were questions in the House about a killer called Christopher Simcox. He had been found guilty of murder at Stafford Assizes, having killed his sister-in-law. He was due to hang on 17 March that year but as *The Times* reported, the Home Secretary had granted a reprieve and the paper explained: 'Mr Brooke did so after receiving a report that Simcox was unable to stand without help, could not walk, had lost about four stones in weight and was under daily medical attention for a self-inflicted stomach wound. The amazing point was that Simcox had been reprieved previously, in 1948, having been given a death sentence for murdering his wife. He was released on licence in 1958. In fact, at that time there had been a hiatus in the continuance of the death penalty because a bill by MP Sidney Silverman had suspended hanging between March and October that year, and Simcox was one of twenty-six people sentenced to die who had sentences commuted.

The saga was to go on, of this man escaping the noose. The Home Secretary even stressed that the reprieve was like any other, and therefore nothing precluded Simcox from the parole process and perhaps release again at some date. It had been a time of heightened activity for the anti-hanging lobby. There had been demonstrations outside the prison at Winson Green, Birmingham. In fact, one person recalled the day of the reprieve, writing that the Governor had spoken to the lobbyists and said, 'I know why you are standing outside and I therefore feel it right to tell you that I have just had notice from the Home Secretary that Simcox is reprieved, and I have so informed him.' The man recalls that the Governor seemed as relieved at the news as the abolitionists were.

The debate then began in earnest. Leo Abse asked the Home Secretary why Simcox had not been recalled to prison at an earlier date, after an attempted murder charge was against him. The prisoner was clearly mentally deranged, so the argument ran: Abse asked why there had been no 'comprehensive medical and psychiatric examination.' There had been a quite stunning mistake made in 1963, after Simcox had been charged with possessing an offensive weapon. Instead of being imprisoned, he had been put on probation. There was no immediate decision to revoke his licence, and the delay meant that a very dangerous man was let loose. The man's prison history was that, after the reprieve of 1948, he had moved through the prison system from a close to an open establishment and then was out on licence. There had been medical reports but there never seemed to have been any action taken on him to protect himself or the public.

The Home Secretary, Brooke, said that in Wakefield Prison, the Principal medical officer in 1957 had said that Simcox was quite fit for open conditions. Then, at Leyhill (a category D open estate) in Gloucestershire, the decision on him made by the doctors was that he was quite normal. Brooke could only say that the advice of professionals had been followed, but that there was a review of psychiatry in prisons being put in motion at that very moment. It all smacks of a rather pathetic attempt to cover up a drastically wrong decision.

Simcox was by trade a maintenance fitter; he was from Smethwick, and there were early signs of a brutality in him that today indicates psychopathic behaviour. He was so cruel to his first wife that their marriage failed. Simcox married again, and then a third time; he was violent and dangerous to those women. After his third wife left, he threatened to kill his wife, went to hunt for her, and succeeded only in shooting dead her sister. He then shot himself twice, but of course, he survived to be tried.

Back in the 1880s, a noted fraudster was sentenced to life imprisonment. His way of escape was to do nothing – to atrophy and waste away, so that he would have to be released on compassionate grounds. He never moved from his bed in Dartmoor. The plan worked; he was released, being in a desperately poor state of health, but he recovered. If it were not for Simcox's mental health problems, it might be thought that he had tried exactly the same ploy.

But here was a man who destined to escape the noose.

A similar fate must have appeared to await Walter Rowland. In 1934, this minder from Derbyshire was sentenced to death after he killed his two-year-old daughter by strangling her with a stocking. In his appeal statement, Rowland had said, 'I am innocent and a victim of circumstances.' In short, the prosecution, it was felt at appeal, never really proved the crime, but that there was enough to persuade the jury of Rowland's guilt. The evidence was seen as purely circumstantial. In the summing up, the judge said, 'It is perfectly clear that the little child has been killed by somebody, that she had been left in the charge of her father … and she was murdered while her mother was elsewhere …'

Stafford courthouse where Simcox was found guilty.

The appeal was dismissed, but Rowland was later reprieved. He served some time and then joined the armed forces. Like Simcox, though, years later, he was once again on a murder charge. This time the scene was Manchester, and the body of prostitute Olive Balchin was found on waste ground in Cumberland Street, Manchester. She had been battered to death with hammer blows to the head. But Rowland was a violent man, and had another conviction as well as the child-murder. He was in Manchester, so he was questioned; he had an alibi that he was at 36 Hyde Road, lodging. In fact his presence had been noted, and he had been signed in on the night of the murder, but that was overlooked. But Rowland admitted that he had been with Olive. He also made several rash statements to the police, including the fact that he had VD and that if it had been Olive who had given him that then she deserved what she got.

Everything was pointing to him as the killer. He was identified on parades, and the times of his stated movements meant that it was just possible for him to have been with Olive at the time she died. He was charged and forensic evidence made things look very black for him, notably the fact that in his trouser turn-ups there was a cluster of materials that matched the same substances at the bomb-site. He was sentenced to death, but then came the stunning news that a man in Walton gaol had confessed to the crime. This was David Ware, and he wrote: 'I wish to confess that I killed Olive Balshaw [that spelling is important] with a hammer at the bombed site in Deansgate, Manchester on Saturday 19 October at about 10 p.m. We had been in a picture house near the Belle Vue stadium.'

This was to prove tantalisingly ambiguous and problematic for the detectives who went to check the man out. The dapper and celebrated Detective Inspector Herbert Hannam of Scotland Yard led the interrogation. Amazingly, Ware gave a detailed account of the night at the pictures, with lots of other details that seemed convincing. Surely that would mean that like Simcox, Rowland was going to be saved from the noose a second time? But Hannam was of the opinion that the details Ware had mentioned could be seen by someone passing by – he did not accept the tale as convincing and thought that Ware was fantasising – being of unsound mind. A report was written for the Home Secretary on Ware's statement. He said his confession was a fabrication: 'I do remember reading in the paper about the peculiarity of the buttons on the coat worn by the murdered woman.' He also finally said, 'I would like to say I am sorry I have given the trouble I have and I didn't realise the serious consequences it might entail had the confession been believed.'

Herbert Hannam reported that he had found a number of press cuttings with details relevant to the case. He wrote: 'In two of these cuttings the victim is said to be "Balshaw". In one of these cuttings published within a few days of the discovery of the body the name is said to be Balshaw ...'

Walter Rowland was hanged at Manchester on 27 February, 1946, by Albert Pierrepoint. He was not as fortunate as Simcox, but between them they had three reprieves and just one hanging. But there is a strange coda to this story; on 10 July, 1951, David Ware tried to kill a woman in Bristol. He had bought a hammer and had tried to batter her to death. He was found guilty but did not hang, for reasons of unsound mind. In fact, he took his own life in Broadmoor, hanging himself in his cell in 1954. Was Rowland innocent after all?

Leslie Hale thought so in his book, *Hanged in Error* (1961) as he says, 'The register at the lodging house where Ware claimed to have spent the Saturday night from about 11.15 onwards had been inspected by two police officers after Ware's confession ... Inspector Hannam went to see it in late February. He was told that the book had been destroyed. The report does not state whether an explanation was asked for or supplied.'

24

A Murderous Attack in Church 1948

Some cases of homicide are particularly complicated with the problem of finding out exactly what the circumstances are that lead to a violent death. If we have a death in which two people struggled and grappled in extreme passion, with no-one else present, then everything in court is going to rest on exactly what went on and who did what. Today, with the modern sophisticated techniques of forensics applied to materials at the scene of the crime, a detailed narrative of events leading to a death may be constructed with scientific support. But sixty years ago, when two women fought in a Dublin church, there was uncertainty as to exactly how the struggle resulted in a death.

The fight happened in the Glasnevin church of Our Lady of the Seven Dolours. The church has now been replaced by a more modern building so again, we have to imagine the scene and its physical environment, but what happened was that Mary Gibbons, who was eighty-three years old and lived in Botanic Avenue, walked to church in August, 1948, as she did every day. She walked on a warm summer day to the dark interior of the church and there she found a pew and began to pray. She was near the confessional, but was completely alone in the church – at least until the door opened again and someone else came in. The door closed after a beam of light had shot in momentarily.

Then we have another woman's story before we find out what happened in the church. Mary Daly was very hard up. Her landlady said that she was living at this time in lodgings with her husband and child, in Botanic Road. They had a struggle to find the weekly rent. Mary had been to beg money from a priest, things were so bad, and he had given her the cash for the week's rent. But it was always going to be a constant battle to survive. In desperation, Mary went to the church in Glasnevin that day, but she had a hammer in her shopping-bag. Her motives will always be a mystery, but the fact is that she went to the church with that potential murder weapon.

As Mary Gibbons prayed she was suddenly aware of a crack on her head. She was a large woman, well-built and still with some strength in spite of her age. After an initial sense of sheer stunned shock she turned to find Mary Daly, who was small and lightly made, wielding a hammer in the light of the church candle. One second she had been saying her *hail Marys* and the next she was fighting for her life.

Mary grabbed Mary Daly's hand and the fight began. Mary Gibbons was bleeding profusely and she broke away and ran to the door of the church to cry for help but more hammer blows were slammed on her head. There was a trail of blood from the pew where the attack began, right to the door.

Some children came to church at that moment and they heard the cries and screams inside, so they decided to run for help and at last, two adults came to try to help. A local butcher called James Canavan and a lorry driver called Thomas Mitchell rushed to the church and they had to force open the door, as one woman was lodged against it. When they forced their way inside, Mitchell immediately realised he had to snatch the hammer from the smaller woman, and he did so, while Canavan tried to help the old lady in her pain. What happened then could have been the scene of any small-scale street brawl in Dublin – something not that uncommon. But it was the beginning of the confusion set before the forces of law in court, because a crowd had gathered, including the children, and what they saw and heard was not a hammer attack from behind but two women screaming, accusing each other of violence.

Old Mary Gibbons naturally told everyone that the younger woman had attacked her, but Daly then retorted with an accusation that Gibbons had tried to rob her and snatch her handbag. Detective Sergeant Joe Turner then arrived and that was the scene of noise and confusion he saw, and in a most unseemly place. An ambulance was called and Turner questioned Daly, who insisted that the old woman had tried to steal her bag. 'I was struggling with her to get my bag back!' she said.

As for Mary Gibbons, who was in hospital as Mary Daly was carried off to the police station, she was very seriously injured. Her skull had several wounds and bones were cracked; but she was able to give evidence in a special court held in the hospital of Mater Misericordiae in Eccles Street. It was to be a period of uncertainty for all concerned, mainly because the victim was confused about the actual events in the church. There was no confidence in her medical condition being either one thing or the other. At first, the doctors thought that she was pulling through and so when Daly stood before Judge O'Flynn on 16 August, the charge was wounding with intent, not attempted murder. But that was to change; at first the old lady was thought to be 'out of danger' but within a day she was dead. Back came Mary Daly to court to face a murder charge.

The trial was on 8 November at the Dublin Central Court. From the accused's home and family situation there came a motive, put together by the counsel for the prosecution, Sir John Esmonde. The financial difficulties of the Daly family (with a young baby to support) meant that facts were uncovered that showed how desperate Mary Daly would be to get hold of some money; there had been a court order served on her to pay her rent. It was in the Church of the Seven Dolours that a priest had given her money just a short time before the attack, so it was an easy matter to find a motive in her return to that church in such dire straits. Was she carrying the hammer in case she had to extort money with threats this time, as opposed to begging and hoping for further largesse from the priest? That seemed to be the case.

The issue was, as there were no witnesses, whether or not Mary Daly went to the church with intent to kill for money or whether there were other reasons for what she had in her bag that day. Testimony from the lorry driver who saw her that day and who restrained her, Mr Mitchell, was that Daly was distressed and excited, and that she did say that the hammer, which she had bought in Woolworths store, was hers; similarly, the children in court, who heard the attack but did not see it, said that they did hear a voice saying 'Help … she's murdering me!' So who was doing the attacking?

Mary Daly was small and the older Mary Gibbons was tall and well-made; that was a factor that complicated things, of course. Daly's defence argument was still that Gibbons had taken the hammer and attacked her; she may have been just five feet two tall and delicately made, but in the end, who had the clear motive? Why would the old lady have attacked Daly? The defence brought in a medical expert to say that the accused was so frail that she could not have used a hammer, and on the matter of her financial straits, Daly said that she did have five pounds on her that day, and that the old lady was intending to steal that from her. The lengthy defence narrative was the familiar one of self-defence; creating a story in which Daly, going into the church for quiet prayer and carrying her bag and purse, was attacked in the semi-darkness and that she happened to have the hammer with her and so she used it. That does not sit easily with the statement that she was too delicate to use a hammer.

The contradictions and confusions continued as Daly claimed that she had only, at first, hit Gibbons on the arm, and that the old lady took the hammer and turned on her; being the stronger, she argued, the old lady then set about whacking her about the body with the weapon. She said, 'I tried to get out the door. I could not as the woman was leaning against it. I kept shouting for my husband for help. I thought I heard footsteps outside. I gave the woman another blow of the hammer on the head ... I did not know where I was hitting her. I hit her to get rid of her.'

The defence really dramatised this situation with great emotional emphasis, saying, 'Anyone who found themselves in Mrs Daly's position would probably have acted as she had done. There was no criminal intent.' But the judge pointed out that Mrs Gibbons had been praying and so that small as she was, Daly would have approached the old lady from a position above. That was a hypothetical detail that had some influence on the jury, who were out to deliberate for an hour or so and came back in with a guilty verdict, though they recommended mercy. But the sentence was one of hanging, with a date fixed in December that year.

The final chapter of this case is one of an incredible series of appeals; a date for appeal was set and then everything depended on points of law, mainly that the deceased had made a formal 'dying declaration' regarding the attack (at that time only one of minor assault, of course) and that such a matter could not be admissible in a murder trial. In an example of what must have been a desperately stressful situation, the judges rejected this but then opened up the possibility of a final appeal to the Supreme Court. There was then a complete re-trial because of legal technicalities, and again the judgement was guilty of murder. For a second time, Mary Daly stood in court and heard her death sentence. But the string of frustrating and dramatic trials ended there, as shortly after that second decision her sentence was commuted to life imprisonment. Mary did a seven-year stretch, followed by time with a religious order, and then went back into her life.

Only very rarely in criminal trials has there been such doubt and uncertainty about the actual events of a case, and the fact that so many people arrived on the scene just a little too late to have any definite evidence on the series of events in the fight only served to make the trial more complex.

25

Legless Man Reprieved 1954

Lincoln prison, on Greetwell Road, north of the city, has experienced some amazing events in its history, including the stunning escape of Irish premier, Eamon de Valera, in February, 1919. But one of the strangest stories is surely the scene in the gaol in November, 1954, when John Docherty was told that he would not hang. He was in the condemned cell awaiting his fate at the hands of the executioner, for the murder of his fiancée, Sybil Hoy in Grantham. What was peculiar about all this was that Docherty had lost both legs as he tried to take his own life on the track in front of a train. Both legs were severed but he survived.

Naturally, in such a case, there would be a sensitive issue at the heart of the death sentence. Although his trial had taken only three minutes before sentence was passed, other factors were to emerge later. In cases of physical deformity, the notion of clemency and common humanity might apply, and a royal pardon be given. The reprieve finally came after the Home Secretary had reviewed the case file. In the end, the point to be debated was how a legless man could be hanged with dignity. In effect, it is the Home Secretary who can choose to exercise the royal prerogative of mercy, on behalf of the Crown.

The circumstances of the murder are that John was engaged to Sybil while they were living in Felling, Durham. The future should have been bright, but partly due to the unhealthy nature of the area they lived in, John contracted tuberculosis and he had to be installed in a sanatorium. He came out and it looked as though he had recovered; but at that time, the prevailing fear and concern about the disease was dominated by the thought that someone with this illness would not really be wise to marry; it could go on through progeny, of course. John unfortunately suffered a relapse and was again hospitalised. The outlook was now sombre and very desperate; time went on and Sybil had other young men paying her attention. John was being left out of her life, and he began to pursue her, to the point of obsession and harassment. She tried to 'disappear' and be beyond contact. But he found her in Grantham and did some detective work to locate her in the town. Sybil was staying in Arnoldfield Flats. On the night of her murder, she walked out into the dark with the three-year-old child of her friend, little Kevin. A neighbour heard screams and Sybil had been beaten and stabbed to death, even while with the little boy. It was a dramatic scene; the push chair was upside down when the neighbour ran to see what was happening.

Docherty was crouching in nearby undergrowth, still with the knife in his hands, and he told the neighbour that he had stabbed her a few times. He then fled. She had, in fact, been stabbed no fewer than nineteen times. It was a frenzied attack by a man who was in a murderous rage of revenge.

Not far off, and a little later, Mr Ernest Bond was working with his colleagues, plate-laying on the railway. They paused when a fast train, going at around 70 mph, rushed past. Seconds after it had gone, Ernest saw something on the like: something he thought was a bundle of clothes. It was Docherty, and his legs had been sliced off. He was rushed to

Grantham hospital, and received all the attention he needed, but by 12 August, the police were at his bedside and he was charged with murder. In Grantham Guildhall, entering in a wheelchair, he was charged and remanded in custody. In Lincoln at the Assizes, he had made a full confession, not only to murder but to having attempted suicide. The latter was a crime at the time, and was so until 1961. He pleaded guilty and was scheduled to hang on 23 November. It was just eight days before that appointment with the scaffold that he was told about the reprieve. The file with 'Urgent-Capital Case' would have been in front of the Home Secretary, and he made a decision that the tabloids had been clamouring for over the previous weeks, as the date of execution was drawing near.

Back in 1907, some of the decisive factors in such decisions had been given by the then Home Secretary, Herbert Gladstone. He had said that, 'The motive, the degree of premeditation or deliberation, the amount of provocation, the state of mind of the prisoner, his physical condition, his character and antecedents ... have to be taken into account in every case.' The judge may have had his own opinion at the time of the sentence, but that could not play a part in the passing of the sentence the criminal law demanded, regardless of the state of the man before him in the dock. Docherty had stated clearly, in explanation that after Sybil left him, 'I did not want to live any more.' She had returned all kinds of presents he had given her, and of course, she had returned his engagement ring. That would have been the final blow. He had no reason to go on living, and his twisted mind thought that she should not live either.

The other factor, however, and it is a very delicate though practical one, is that the professionals who would have had to deal with Docherty in the execution suite at the prison would have been asked to go through a demeaning experience. The prison officers, the chaplain, the governor and indeed the hangman, would have found the notion of hanging a legless man not only absurd but unethical. As to whether the man was of sound mind at the time of the killing, well, yes. He had planned to murder Sybil. But then his attempted suicide was as planned as the murder, so the whole narrative leading to his discovery on the railway line has a tough relentless logic about it. The man who wanted to die that night in front of a train may well have had the same death-wish in the prison, but the mode of exit from his life there was surely entirely different from the suicide he wanted; giving someone else the task was too much. The 'system' could not cope with that responsibility, and the media played a part in that dilemma.

Docherty was not the only reprieve case that year; in 1953, five of the eighteen people sentenced to die were reprieved. As to Docherty's sentence, he was to serve not less than fifteen years. The most relieved man in Lincoln on that day when the waited-for news arrived at HMP Lincoln was surely the governor, William Harding. As to the hangman, he must have been delighted that he had been deprived of the practical problem of how one pinions such a man, and how the 'drop' would be calculated accurately.

If we look for comparisons to this strange tale and the act of taking men to execution who are ill or in some way deficient or unsuitable for facing the experience, perhaps the strongest parallel is a political one, because in Kilmainham gaol, Dublin, after the Easter rebellion of 1916, James Connolly was taken out to face a firing squad; he was on a stretcher and had been taken from a bed in the Castle Hospital before he was carried into the stone-breaking yard to be despatched to the next world. The comparison only serves to illustrate that, when it comes to trying to understand the nature of capital punishment through modern eyes, there is no point in looking for consistency in the routes by which men and women arrived at their fatal appointments at the hands of the state. The inconsistent and often brutal chronicle of twentieth century capital

The legless man reprieved.

punishment will always be found to have dozens of stories like this of Docherty; at the centre of these dramas there are always the circumstances of the individual case, and this is invariably at odds with the letter of the law. Not only did questions of insanity and sanity raise difficult moral issues in court, but contrasts of crimes done in different 'arenas' of crime caused problems.

Docherty's case illustrates the paradox of a person wanting to end his or her own life and then, with altered times and new frames of mind, their position changes and the state steps in to decide their fate. Not surprisingly, in this case, the popular media made a sensation of the affair, and in the annals of murder, this will always be simply the 'legless man story.' Beneath this, there is a desperately melancholy tale of a man, like Othello, who loved, 'Not wisely, but too well' and jealousy led to the old formula for the crime of passion: 'If I can't have her, then nobody else will either.'

26

The Widow of Windy Nook 1957

In the 1950s, phosphorus was used in the manufacture of rat poison. It had been essential to the production of matches for many decades and the match-makers had suffered all kinds of disabling illnesses through handling it. Although it could be used as a poison by a murderer, the instances of it having been used as an instrument of death are quite rare. The north east has the dubious distinction of being home to one of the most shameless and nasty poisoners to use this deadly stud – Mary Elizabeth Wilson from Windy Nook, Felling-on-Tyne.

Phosphorus is a very powerful killer – one grain of it is all it takes to harm the liver, cause horrific convulsions and then a fatal coma. So potent is this material that, in a case of 1991, in Perth, Australia, when a suicide's corpse was being moved, it dripped lethal substances and fumes. The man had used phosphorus to kill himself.

Over the centuries in English social history, the most obvious choices for poisoning a victim were arsenic and antimony as both were commonly used around the house. Various laws had later restricted the use of such poisons but phosphorus was used in the rat poison, Rodine. It was a simple matter for someone to mix a paste from this and to place it in something like jam or chutney. Only four years before Mary Wilson appeared in the dock on a murder charge, in Liverpool, Louisa Merrifield had used phosphorus with rum to kill her employer, Mrs Ricketts. Merrifield was hanged. Wilson's case was to become notorious, partly because the famous forensic scientist, Francis Camps, was to come north to give evidence.

Wilson's affection for the act of murder most probably began when she realized what an easy way to make money the crime could be. Everything about her life and her general appearance suggested a plain, everyday person. She was known to be fond of reading romantic fiction, yet her relationships and her attitudes to husbands and lovers were anything but sentimental or affectionate. Her first husband was a labourer, one John Knowles, but she also had a lover, a chimney-sweep called John Russell. She had begun to work as a domestic servant and that was how she met her first husband. But clearly she wanted money to flow towards her without the necessity for hard graft. In a period of only five months, both the husband and the lover died.

This was an age when older residents – and these men were much older than Mary – had a life expectancy much shorter than today. This meant that 'natural causes' was almost an everyday phrase to the average GP when faced with yet another death. Mary inherited a total of £46 from the two deaths. That would have sustained her in some comfort for a year maybe, adding a little pocket money for luxuries. We know little of any certainty about these two deaths, but it is what happens next that shows Mary becoming much bolder in her murderous proclivities.

She married a man much older than she was – by now she was sixty-four, and her new husband, Oliver Leonard, was seventy-five. He was in lodgings in Hebburn at the time they met and, in a later testimony given at the trial, it was stated that Mary had brazenly said to the landlord, 'Has the old bugger any money?' This attitude and a twisted sense of black humour were to be the hallmarks of her foul life story.

When they first got together, they shared lodgings, but Wilson wanted to secure an inheritance so they married in Jarrow in 1957. Anyone who had known Mary Wilson's track record would have been suspicious when, only weeks after the wedding, the old husband caught a bad chill and also became remarkably weak and fragile, as if his constitution had degenerated alarmingly quickly. A neighbour, Mrs Ellen Russell, was called out by Mary one night in an appeal for help because Oliver was so ill. She found the poor man lying on the floor, in great pain and struggling to move. Mary had not called a doctor. All Russell could do was offer tea, and real significance was read into the fact that the desperate Oliver threw his away – had he been poisoned by something in his tea? The two women felt that the man was going to die and it was recorded by Russell that Mary had said, 'I've called you because you'll be handy if he dies.'

Oliver was an old man who had lived a hard life and, as with the first two men, the doctor merely saw this as death due to heart failure and consequently considered the cause of death to be heart disease and chronic nephritis. With his death, the widow added another £50 to her savings – but this was not to be enough. The habit of chasing older men and worming her way into their affections was obviously lucrative, and she had the urge to carry on. Her next target was Ernest Wilson, a man of the same age as Oliver. He proposed to her not long after they met and we now know that he had a Co-op investment of £100 and rented a shabby council house – not a great catch, but then Mary was not ambitious for a larger scale of investment and profit just yet. Small sums suited her fine.

This time she was cannier. Whereas before she had plunged in recklessly and relied on the fact of the victim's age being enough to satisfy the local doctor, this time she saw to it that, when the new husband became ill, she went to the doctor with him. He was ordered to bed, and sure enough, within a day, he was dead. Remarkably, although the man's condition rapidly worsened, she never sent for the doctor again – and as before, the doctor saw nothing suspicious in this and put it down to his age and slowness of actions. After the wedding to Ernest, she had held a party and told the caterer to save any leftover cakes, saying, 'They will come in handy for a funeral.' This sick humour continued, right up to the time of her arrest. She also said that she had not killed the first two husbands as they were 'dead already.'

Their corpses were exhumed and pathologists, rather than the family doctors, inspected the bodies and 'natural causes' were certainly not found. Phosphorus is not a natural constituent of the human body – it is yellow and the yellowness stays for some time. Dr David Price pronounced that both men had died 'in the first stage of phosphorus poisoning.'

Mary had a talented defence lawyer in Rose Heilbron, and Heilbron saw that, given the damning scientific evidence, the case was going to be a very difficult one to defend. The men had been of advanced age but there was general medical agreement that phosphorus had been used, most likely in cough medicine or in tea. Heilbron needed help if she was to stand any chance of saving her client from the gallows.

Enter Francis Camps, an acknowledged expert on poisons and a man with a formidable medical reputation. Camps was a man of real presence and gravity – he was smart, proper and disciplined. He had been one of the men who founded the British Association of Forensic Medicine in 1950. Born to a medical family in 1905, he gathered valuable experience in Essex hospitals and then in the army. He knew, however, what he wanted to do for his career – forensics. He gradually put together a laboratory and steadily gained an enviable reputation.

This was the man now standing in the courtroom and Heilbron needed him to put some shred of doubt in the minds of the jury. He stated that he was sure that phosphorus had been used in the Wilson cases but, being of a sound scientific mind, he asserted that 'it would be dangerous to say that it was phosphorus gas [that caused the deaths] because other causes of death have not been excluded.'

Camps then noted that the pathological causes of death in both cases were 'contradictory' and it was his theory that both jam and cough medicine had perhaps been used as agencies for the administration of the deadly paste. This was crucially important, as the method of administering the poison was in need of verification. One useful detail ascertained by Heilbron's questioning was that Rodine alone would not have been administered. As Camps said, 'A person would have to be blind and without taste or smell. There is a cloud of vapour as soon as you open the tin. The taste is horrible.' But could it still have been the cause of these deaths?

Heilbron knew that there was a chance to introduce an element of doubt into the trial. She put forward another possible cause of death – these were old men and the incidence of death in men of that age in that social context was very high. The use of the branded rat poison was very common. Also, was not phosphorous an unlikely substance for a woman to have used?

In the end, although Camps would not state openly that phosphorus was the definite cause of the deaths, there was no other apparent cause. There had been no 'nephritis' [death-moribund cells] of tissue and the hearts in question had been healthy. On balance the probability was that there had been deliberate poisoning.

The prosecution suggested Wilson had lied and she had planned the murders. There had been some hilarity in the court when her defence countered this by saying that pills used as sexual aids might have been a factor (much as the Victorians were fond of using tiny traces of arsenic for the same purpose). Just a few years before Wilson was tried, there had been the Merrifield case, so it was not unheard of. Wilson was then found guilty on two counts of murder. However, she was not to hang for the offences as she was considered too old for that fate. The killer went to prison and died there when she was seventy years old. The case had highlighted the fact that family doctors were in the habit of attributing somewhat vague causes of death in old people at the time, a fact that Mary Wilson had exploited to the full.

27

Two Stories from the Suburbs

I have left these two until last because they have the most complex and fascinating denouement, and the events happened in the steel town in North Lincolnshire, Scunthorpe, hardly a place associated with such sensational stories.

The steel town of Scunthorpe had its problems with crime in the 1930s, along with every other place in which there was immigrant labour, poverty and social divisions of rich and poor. But in 1937, the big news in the town was of a killing in a quiet street just a few hundred yards away from the police court. But this was no death during a robbery and no mugging. Just after Christmas 1936, Mrs Doris Teasdale shot her husband with a gun he kept under a mattress.

Cecil Teasdale was a butcher, 29 years old, and Doris just a year younger. Cecil liked to stay out late and he enjoyed the company of other women. There had been stresses and strains in the marriage for some time and to make things worse, their first son, just four years old, had died not long before. On the fateful morning, Cecil came down to eat his breakfast and then a maid heard the conversation. The husband saw Doris with the gun and told her to stop fooling. 'I'm not fooling' she said. Then a shot was fired and Doris ran out in a panic, screaming for help. A doctor was called and a neighbour came to try to help. Cecil was not dead, but severely wounded.

Everything in their story points to a tragic accident and this is what the court decided, but it was a close-run thing. Doris was sure that the gun only had blanks, and her husband had told her so not long before. In court, Doris Teasdale had to prove that she had no intention of killing her husband, but that she was intending only to frighten him. At the trial in Lincoln, the famous Mr Justice Travers Humphreys presided, and he put his finger on the legal dilemma: 'If this is the truth it is highly dangerous and most unlawful for any person to fire a revolver in the neighbourhood of another person.' In court, then, lawyers had to probe her real feelings towards her husband, who had taken several days to die in hospital. Mr Richard O'Sullivan prosecuted, and he moved in with the relevant questions, asking if she were 'reckless in this matter if the gun were loaded.' She had taken a gun she knew to be loaded, but that she was convinced there were blanks in it. She said that she was 'fooling' not in the sense of taking the gun to him but in picking it up at all.

The famous Norman Birkett defended, and he drew out her feelings with care and directness: 'When you married your husband you were very much in love with him?'
Witness: Very deeply.
Birkett: Did that love for your husband never die?
Witness: Never.
Birkett: When you found that he was with other women, staying out ... why didn't you leave him?
Witness: Because I loved him too much for that.

When their child had died, Cecil had been out until two in the morning. As Birkett said, 'It was during the week that he lay dying.'

Doris told the court that she went towards the room that morning with the thought of just scaring her husband.

But she stood there and brandished the weapon. When he saw her he had said, 'Stop fooling Dot' and then, 'Oh well, it doesn't matter. It's loaded with blanks.' But before a shot was fired they talked in an animated way about where he had been and why he stayed out. She tried reasoning with him, and she told Birkett that she had never become enraged at the time.

So we have a situation in which a person entered a room carrying a gun with the intention of causing fear, not causing grievous bodily harm and certainly not murder. But it was a tough job sorting out why both murder and manslaughter should be discounted.

They had had a second child, born just over a year before these events, having married in 1927 in Lincoln; they were happy until, around 1932, Mr Teasdale took a new shop. Things became notably unsteady and sometimes rocky. There were testimonies about their having quarrels – something Doris denied. 'They were more arguments than quarrels', she said.

But through the eyes of the law, the delicacy of the situation was summed up by Humphreys: 'The law of this country is jealous of the lives of its citizens, so jealous that to take the life of another citizen done without consent of that citizen is murder … or to take a life by negligently firing a gun which turns out to be loaded is at least manslaughter.'

On the face of things, it must have seemed as though manslaughter was a strong possibility. After all, what she did could easily be interpreted as 'reckless' and of course, she took the gun with 'negligence' as to the real facts of the case. What turned matters in her favour was evidence that Mr Teasdale, not long before, had fired a chamber, saying that there were merely blanks there, and then being astonished when a bullet was fired.

O'Sullivan puts things boldly: 'My submission is that she is at least guilty of manslaughter …' But as the truth of their lives together came through, sympathy was gathered for Mrs Doris Teasdale, partly through the bereavement she had suffered, and for the stoical way she dealt with the adultery. But mostly, her ignorance of firearms was obvious and all the witnesses testifying to words she spoke immediately after the shooting confirmed this. They also confirmed the view that she was genuinely shocked at what had happened. The gun, clearly fired with the intention of firing a blank well wide of the man, had juddered and he had been hit. He died of peritonitis; the bullet had broken a rib and entered the abdomen, and then the peritonitis set in.

Because Teasdale was often out for so long and he tended to leave the garage doors open, he kept a gun to scare any intruders. That was reckless, of course; so some of his habits tended to add to the opinion of Doris as a hapless victim of his lifestyle and odd ways that developed in court. Not only did she have a young child and had been a long-suffering wife, she had also, it was said, been cruelly treated in custody. Her lawyer had found her in a pitiful state in the police cell, as the local newspaper reported: 'Mr Lewes wished to make a strong protest against the accommodation provided at Scunthorpe for a woman on remand …'

The sympathy piled up; the human story came through, a tale of tragic proportions and without doubt the tale of a long-suffering woman whose actions on that day had been thoughtless and foolish rather than malevolent.

By January 16, the townspeople of Scunthorpe had raised a defence fund for Doris Teasdale amounting to £350 – a very large sum at that time. She was on remand at Hull prison at the time, and a local butcher, Tom Fisher, after consulting Mr T. J. Lewis, her solicitor, had taken charge of that fund-raising. He did a great job, even announcing the campaign on local cinema screens. It was known that she had no money and a good 'brief' was desired for her. She got the very best: Norman Birkett K. C.

In the biography of Birkett by Montgomery Hyde, it is noted that Birkett's opinion was reiterated; he had said, 'When you are dealing with the important question of intent, consider her attitude in the box. There was no venom. It was plain she never intended to do the slightest harm to her husband. The atmosphere of that room was not threatening ...'

Doris Teasdale stood in the dock on 12 February 1937; a frail, pathetic figure. It was noted that she stood 'pale but composed' between two women warders.

Mr Justice Humphreys took over an hour to sum up; he was confident that the jury should settle on the decision of manslaughter. That would, of course, have been expected after such a direction from his eminence.

But those present were in for a surprise, as it was reported at the time:

'The jury, absent for two hours and ten minutes, disagreed and to the relief and astonishment of an eagerly awaiting court, they returned a verdict of not guilty on both charges.'

The young woman 'sobbed for an hour' in between thanking her legal team. After that she disappeared into the rural calm of Lincolnshire, 'reunited with her sixteen-month-old baby.' As for Cecil Walter Teasdale, he was buried at Brumby Cemetery, Scunthorpe. He had died in Scunthorpe War Memorial Hospital. Some say the truth was buried with him; others are convinced that the legal outcome was the right one. The house still stands – just a small house in a quiet street near the town centre – still hiding its dark secrets.

The centre of Scunthorpe, even today when so much as changed, has housing in long terraces of red brick, with gaps between called 'ten-foots' locally. In the early and mid-twentieth century, these warrens of side streets and back alleys, close to where large numbers of people were living so close to each other, were scenes of close family ties, but also of some nasty crime and many townsfolk were vulnerable. Old people, women alone at night and anyone seen to be weak and an easy target for robbery were notably open to assault, and as with every other town with casual labour and a transient element in the population, trouble in the streets was not uncommon.

In the 1950s for instance, people living in those streets made sure that doors were locked and back gates made secure. Such a careful person was sixty-nine-year-old Emily Charlesworth, a housekeeper at number 4, Ravendale Street. But on 23 September, 1945, all her care about self-protection came to nothing, as she was found battered to death in her kitchen. She worked as live-in housekeeper for steelworker Harry Ramshaw, and had been in that capacity for many years. Emily was born in Scunthorpe, and was an active church worker, and as the *Evening Telegraph* reported at the time, she was 'known in the neighbourhood as a quiet, unassuming woman' who had 'worked for some years as nursemaid to a clergyman's family in Australia.' She had come home to Scunthorpe twenty-seven years before, in 1918.

Ramshaw found her body when he returned from the night-shift at six in the morning, after leaving his home at nine-thirty the previous evening to be on time for the ten o'clock shift. He found her body in the kitchen, the gas light being still on. Police initially reported that there had been no signs of a struggle and that Ramshaw thought no money had been stolen. But it later emerged that a blood-stained bread knife was found that that is was likely that Emily tried to defend herself.

From the very beginning, these factors were to make this a puzzling case, as the death was the result of extreme violence and the motive was not clear. Unusually, the back door of the house was unlocked and there were pots on the table, and as she had been entertaining a guest she had not changed into any new clothes, as she still wore her working-clothes.

Ravendale Street at that time was surrounded by other dwellings, bordered by an optician and a services canteen. The kitchen faced onto the back yard and the ten-foot, the latter still existing today, though Ramshaw's house is now part of a shop, and bricked-in windows that were part of number four may still be seen. An important detail is that the sitting room was visible from the main thoroughfare of Ravendale Street.

A post-mortem was carried out by Dr J. M. Webster of the Home Office and this was not available at the inquest on 24 September, so at that stage witnesses were called, and the high drama unfolded across the town as people read that top Scotland Yard officers were in town. Chief Inspector Davis and Sergeant Wolf were present, alongside Scunthorpe man Superintendent Knowler. The coroner then gave more details, describing the state of Emily Charlesworth when found, with her head severely battered. Her face was so badly damaged that Ramshaw only recognised her by means of her green jumper and the shape of her figure. The niece, Edna Warner, was also present.

Harry Ramshaw talked about his last words to Emily as he left for work; she had said it was time for him to catch his bus and then she said, 'Do be careful Harry.' This was a reference to the risks involved in his work.

Clearly, attention turned to whether or not there might have been a visitor to Emily that evening. Her niece and Harry both said that this was unlikely. Edna Warner made a point of saying how happy and cheerful her aunt had been about a month earlier when she had last seen her. Even so early in the investigation, there were difficulties, and all the police could say was that they were following a line of enquiry. The pathologist's report was desperately needed.

Meanwhile, a fingerprint expert, CI Birch, and a crime scene photographer, DI Law, also came north from the Yard. The whole enquiry was escalating. The local reports were fragmented at this early stage, and papers were eager to snap up any little detail. Some said that a neighbour had heard a scream; another that a vital clue had been found but was not sure what that was. The coroner, Mr Dyson, was told by Knowler that it would be some weeks before the police were in a position to pass on any definitely important information.

Meanwhile, as a significant development broke on 26 September, the Scunthorpe public had just one image of the poor woman who had died so violently; a photograph taken of her outside the Ravendale home when she was much younger. The girl in the photograph is thin and spare, with long arms, short hair and a warm, playful expression on her face. She wears a sleeveless summer dress. No doubt this was Emily back in 1918.

Still with no real forensic details, the vagueness of the murder was still predominant in the reports, but two details were released; first, a beer bottle had been found in the house, and then accounts of a courting couple being in the ten-foot near the house were given. The local report was speculation, raising the dramatic level of the events:

'A further clue – a stout bottle found on the scene of the crime has been revealed today. The police are making an urgent appeal to customers of a local hotel to inform them of any instance of a person seen taking away a Guinness bottle on Saturday night. The bottle may have an important bearing on the case.'

The reporter also supposed that Emily was 'unconscious when the fatal blows were struck.' The speculation would have brought in appeals to four local pubs, all within a few hundred yards of the Ravendale Street house. The closest one was on the next block along from Ravendale Street. But of course, there was also the neighbouring services canteen, and police thinking linked the man in the courting couple to the army. There was apparently a sighting and it seems likely. This makes sense when we consider the wider context; men were being demobbed steadily after the end of the war. Hiroshima and Nagasaki had been bombed only seven weeks before this murder and in stages, servicemen were coming home, many to no work and some to a rootless existence; logically, the police would be thinking in terms of tracking down demobbed men, as Emily's home was so close to a place where these men would gather. The ten-foot passageways in the town were then and are still places where lovers meet, and where youngsters gather. The ten-foot by the murder house is sprayed with graffiti today.

The next stage was to scale down the level of fear and panic in the town. People were assured that there was no 'homicidal maniac' on the loose, and as with most murder cases, in the gaps between solid information and developments in the investigation, all kinds of wild stories surfaced. One of the strangest in Scunthorpe was the arrival of a note at the police station from a local medium. This lead to the headline: 'Was Murderer Drowned?' The medium claimed she had been 'talking' to the killer, and that he was a serviceman expecting release, that he had been to the old lady's home and that she had made him tea. The mysterious communication of the killer claimed to describe running away 'in a terrific wind' after the killing, and goes on:

'I don't know where I went, but eventually I came to a pond, or water in a dyke. I may have been near the Trent. I just jumped into it. Make it known if you can to those who have it in hand. I was fully dressed so cannot be far away. I would rather not give you my name.'

With quiet irony, the reporter noted that 'The police have interviewed the spiritualist.'

Meanwhile, Emily Charlesworth's body was laid to rest at St John's church in the town, a church she had attended all her life except when abroad. There was a huge crowd outside, and when the Rev. Swaby had completed his sermon and kind words about the woman, the coffin was carried out and a hush descended on the crowd. The *Evening Telegraph* noted that the Scotland Yard men were present, and that 'There was a crowd at the gates of Brumby cemetery when the cortège arrived. At the western end a number of women, some of them with young children standing in front of them, had already lined up near the open grave and only the arrival of the funeral party ... induced them to move back.' In short, the case was dominating local conversation and there was a sense of outrage. They were saying goodbye to a woman who 'did a lot of small jobs in a very thorough way' as Rev. Swaby said. A woman who sold tickets for church events, kept a clean house and cared for her employer was noteworthy for being ordinary, and so the sense of disgust and revulsion grew.

This was to play a part in the next stage of the investigation. Meanwhile, the search went on for clues or materials in the area. Every house in Scunthorpe and the nearby villages was subject to enquiry and questioning about possible witnesses or sightings of the army man. Five hundred people were interviewed, and the appeal for the courting couple to come forward was sustained. A cryptic announcement was placed in the press about this lead: 'The police believe it is possible that one or other of the couple may have personal reasons for not wishing to reveal their presence in the ten-foot in those circumstances. In that case the companion may come forward and may do so without hesitation. Information from only one of the couple would satisfy the police.'

The soldier wanted for questioning was now shaping up into some kind of profile and police communicated that the man was in Oswald-Road on the night of the murder, and had been seen again in the town since. Oswald-Road is only half a mile from the Ramshaw home. He was aged between twenty-five and thirty, about five feet nine inches tall with a pale complexion and large eyes. He had been seen wearing a khaki raincoat and carrying a valise. That would have guaranteed that the man would leave town, and if he did, he would have most probably been seen, but nothing came of it. When October arrived and there was still no real progress, the Scotland Yard men tried to allay fears and announced that rumour-mongering and 'hysteria' would not help. But by 2 October, the courting couple had been found.

There were now definite clues being considered, and from the kitchen where the body was found; the blood-stained bread knife, the Guinness bottle and the blood found on a pair of fire-irons. It was only when attention given to the lovers was forgotten and the sensational news that Harry Ramshaw had been charged with the murder that these earlier material details of the scene of the crime came back into the foreground.

Two detectives, Kirby and Davis, had interviewed Ramshaw at Scunthorpe police station, and he had been charged. Ramshaw, unsteady and shocked as he came into the magistrate's court to face the charge, was smart, wearing a blue suit, and he could only say, 'I have told Inspector Davis all I know.' But the full wording of the charge must have been forbidding for this simple, hard-working man: 'On the 22 of September, in the parish of Scunthorpe, feloniously, wilfully and of his malice aforethought did kill and murder Emily Jane Charlesworth, against the peace of our sovereign lord the King, his crown and dignity.'

Ramshaw was shocked; he had made no arrangements for legal aid and he wept as he asked for advice. He was given representation and then led away by two officers.

When the appearance at the police court was made again, a few weeks later, a fuller picture of the whole affair was to emerge. First, the pathologist's report was now summarised; the attack had been brutal in the extreme. Not a single bone in her face was unbroken. Dr Webster was sure that Emily had fought against her attacker, and that she had also been strangled. On the other hand, the first of many details about Ramshaw that were to question the whole process of his interrogation and arrest began to emerge. Dr Collins had inspected Ramshaw and found that there were no signs of any injury on him; no abrasions or cuts.

Before the magistrates chaired by John Tomlinson, the story of what Ramshaw had done that awful night was given. A neighbour had seen him come out onto the street at six on the Sunday morning; he was crying and saying that his housekeeper was dead. Mr Claxton, prosecution, said that the neighbour, Mr Dennis, 'could not get much sense out of him, as he was obviously upset.' Ramshaw then went to the home of her niece in Ethel Street, which was on the end of Cole Street, just a few hundred yards from Ravendale Street. The niece was Miss Thompson; she came and then phoned the police. Emily was lying on her back with her arms and legs stretched out.

After seven, Sergeant Ogilvie arrived and he saw that Ramshaw was terribly upset. The scene in the kitchen was a bloodbath. One of the woman's shoes was sticking in blood by the fireplace and blood was splashed on the wall. There was also blood on her stocking-knees. All Ramshaw said was that he spoke to her and she did not speak, that was when he came in from his night shift. The mess in the room was horrendous; the woman's dentures were on the floor, and her glasses were jammed in her hair, with one lens in blood by the side of her head. A bent brass poker lay under the table. Both a sharp instrument and a blunt instrument had been used on her broken face. The bruises on her hands made it clear that she had tried to fend off blows coming at her face; she had died by strangulation.

Emily Charlesworth's last day alive had been normal; after doing most of her housework, she had been visited by Miss Naughton, and they had had a chat in the living room until the visitor left around quarter past four. Emily was standing at her front door at six-thirty that evening, and was seen there by a Mrs Cooper. Her friends, giving statements, described the way in which Emily always took precautions to keep the property secure; her habit was to lock the back gate by the ten-foot, lock the back door, and even put a brick under the gate. 'She was not fond of strangers' one woman said.

On 27 September, CI Davis had started his series of interviews with Ramshaw, and had made the man take him to the murder scene and go through his movements and responses on the morning when he found the body. On 2 October he was interviewed again. At that point he was charged with the murder. He had been under considerable pressure and had asked to go home, but was detained.

In court, Ernest Dennis, an engine driver, confirmed that as he came home from work that morning he saw Ramshaw in tears. 'He was crying, shaking all over and was very agitated. He told Dennis that his housekeeper was dead and that he did not know what to do. He asked Dennis for help. He said that he was sure she was dead because there was blood all over her face. Another neighbour was a valuable witness too: Ellen Foulston who lived at number eight in the street. She awoke at just before six and she saw and heard Ramshaw and Dennis outside; she heard Ramshaw say, 'Something terrible has happened to my housekeeper.' She went outside and spoke to them, offering to help. The doctor came and all four people went inside. Again, Foulston confirmed that Ramshaw was 'sobbing.' Ravendale Street is not long; then, the houses were huddled close together and all street noises would easily have been heard. Living two houses away, though, Foulston would not have heard noises from inside number four. She said she had heard nothing unusual when asked in court.

What was the relationship between Ramshaw and Emily? This was becoming increasingly important now that Ramshaw was in the spotlight and charged. Miss Thompson was asked for her opinion and said that 'Ramshaw and Miss Charlesworth were very fond of each other.' They have lived a routine life, like a couple, and were both very supportive and co-operative. Ramshaw was an industrious man, doing hard physical work. Emily had an established routine and had a busy life with church work and housekeeping, with a few close friends.

Dr Collins' evidence about his examination of Ramshaw was to prove crucially important. When he did the examination, four days after the killing, he found remarkable in connection with the attack: 'On his chest, arms, forearms, legs, head, face and hands there were no signs of injury, abrasions or bruises.' He agreed with the pathology report that there had been a desperate struggle for life against the murderer, and that marks would logically be expected on the body of the attacker. His first statement about the time of the attack was to prove important; he said that it occurred at around ten hours before his examination – and that would place the time of the murder at about eight in the evening of the Saturday.

From 23 October, when Ramshaw's defence counsel began their work, some murky waters were stirred in court, and with the Scotland Yard men in focus. T. J. Lewis, for Ramshaw, probed into the words and attitudes generally applied when Ramshaw was questioned. He brought up mention of 'the noose' waiting for the suspect, and some allegation of torment involving the words, 'I have a good mind to strangle *you*.' But basically Ramshaw had said that when he came home on the Sunday morning he had found the gate and back door open. The back door key had been on the lock inside. At that point, Ramshaw began to crack in court. He was an emotional wreck, and when a relative of Emily's took the stand, another side of Ramshaw's character began to be visible.

This was Mr McGlone, and he spoke of Ramshaw's mental state and learning difficulties: 'Why Harry, you remember what happened before auntie's death. You want to be man and not have the mind of a child.' The story coming from the Yard men after this, concerning their interrogation of Ramshaw, is very questionable; Davis drove Ramshaw to the house, then in the car they had a conversation which suggests that Ramshaw was under extreme pressure and was becoming confused and apprehensive. He shook hands with the detective, said, 'I wish all this could be over' and then he was told that after a night's rest he would be questioned again. Ramshaw allegedly then said, 'I cannot remember touching her ... I do not want to go down the line of get a life sentence for it ... I cannot remember what I have done ...' Defence stepped in swiftly and insisted that these words were not the voluntary words used by the accused man. This was to lead to some very serious allegations against the Yard officers.

Other details which were part of the case against Ramshaw disappeared. The Guinness bottle for instance; the prosecution had found it very strange that no fingerprints of Ramshaw were found at all in the room. But then referring to the prints, CI Davis was questioned by Lewis for the defence:

Lewis: Are you suggesting that in telling the court of that last suspicion of yours that the accused had removed all traces of finger prints from every and any article in the room after the crime?
Davis: I make no suggestion.
Lewis: Is not that the logical conclusion? Some persons might infer that.

The course of the trial was turning in Ramshaw's favour, and facts such as the landlord of the Oswald Hotel saying that he had never seen Ramshaw in the pub at any time, and that there were no prints matching Ramshaw's on the bottle, gathered more doubts about the guilt of the accused.

The focus then shifted to the mental state of Ramshaw, as hinted at by the nephew of Emily Charlesworth. Lewis fastened onto this, and faced the detective with the delicate nature of how Ramshaw should be described. He asked if the officer would describe the accused as being mentally retarded, and the reply was, 'I would not go so far as to say that. I am not a mental expert. I should say he was slightly backward.' This became a grilling, aimed at finding out how Ramshaw had been treated when questioned.

Lewis: I put it to you that he was a worn-out, tired man after the gruelling by Sergeant Wolf and you?

Davis: I was probably more worn-out myself.

Lewis then referred to the showing of the scene of the crime photos to Ramshaw, and made it seem like mental torture. Ramshaw had said that when he made his statement, he was sandwiched between Davis and Wolf, and that he was 'a nervous wreck' at the time.

Lewis was out to show the jury that there was a possibility that the Yard men had used some tough tactics on a man with mental health problems. There had allegedly been provoking questions about a noose waiting for Ramshaw, and that a courting couple outside the house had heard him quarrelling with Emily. It is not difficult to picture the scene: two men applying tough and aggressive interrogation techniques to a man who is already distraught and weary, becoming more and more confused as time goes on. The detective denied saying that 'the noose is getting tighter and tighter' to the accused, and denied mentioning strangling to torment him.

The final ploy by the defence was to tackle the question of Ramshaw's statement.

Lewis: Was the statement the result of questions put by you to the accused?

Davis: No Sir.

Lewis: And of course, when you had got the answers, you had solved the riddle?

Davis: No Sir.

Lewis: Why not?

Davis: I was hoping to get corroborative evidence.

Lewis: And have you got any?

Davis: No.

Lewis: And there is nothing in the statement which tells you how he committed the crime?

Davis: No, Sir.

Lewis knew that the prosecution case was cracking and he was going for the most vulnerable and contentious element in the police officers' actions as reported by his client. It was not a difficult task, but it needed handling with care and sensitivity. He sensed the opposition in retreat.

The prosecution had to answer all this, and Mr Claxton for the Crown said that the statement was admissible and that under judges' rules it was possible to submit these things if a man was suspected. This refers to the written guidance given to police before the changes brought about by the Police and Criminal Evidence Act of 1984. There was room for manoeuvre in these, and also room for exploitation and bias when circumstances were desperate in the urge to make an arrest. These rules were notoriously flexible, and could be adapted to suit anyone at any time with the right degree of resolve and teamwork. The very words make the concept quite formal and formidable when spoken by a police officer.

But one aspect had not been touched on: Harry Ramshaw at work. Fred Cullen, of Ferry Road, worked with Ramshaw as a skip-filler at Lysaghts works, and he confirmed that Ramshaw came to work just after 10 p.m. on the night of the murder. He had worked with Ramshaw all night, until Cullen left for home at around 5.40 the next morning. What came out of this testimony was not only an alibi, but a perspective on

Harry Ramshaw that added a great deal to an accurate picture of his personality being assembled in court. Cullen noted that Ramshaw was 'a quiet man and never joined in conversation in the cabin, and he was just the same as usual that night.' Harry Ramshaw was a man of regular habits and entirely reliable; he took cold tea to work, in a pint bottle. On the night in question, he had behaved entirely normally. It was clear to everyone in the court room that Ramshaw would be cleared.

On 4 November, he was acquitted at Lincoln Assizes. The supposed 'confession' was totally discredited and Mr Justice Denning directed the jury with the words, 'You have no alternative. You must find this man not guilty.' What could be more simple and yet more telling than the fact that, in spite of the gargantuan struggle that had taken place in the kitchen, with the victim's blood in so many places, there had been no blood on any of Ramshaw's clothing, and no marks or signs of a fight on his body? He was the last person to see Emily alive; that is all that may be said. Otherwise, all his behaviour had been entirely in keeping with a man who had just lost his dearest friend, and there was no motive whatsoever in his killing her; it made sense to no-one; the man had an alibi, and there was no material evidence of his being in a tough physical confrontation.

In Lincoln, this was a major attraction for the public, as the participation of the Scotland Yard men, and the unresolved nature of the accused's mental condition had attracted the attention of the popular media. A very long queue had gathered in Lincoln waiting to enter the public gallery. The first stage of the events was that the all-male jury had to retire, as the depositions about the nature of the confession had to be stated and presented. A further addition to the defence case was an appraisal by the prison medical officer about Ramshaw, in which the opinion was expressed that the man 'had an intelligence which was below average – the equivalent of a child of eleven years and three months.' The issue was the procedure that took place before the interview with Ramshaw: here he was told to take notes on what he saw before the detective saw him. Defence said that this might have had an effect on the man which it would not have done on a normal adult. The defence team had done an excellent job of work.

The judge expressed the central point of contention in this way: 'Confession or no confession the Crown must prove the case. If I had to disregard the evidence of the Chief Inspector I would find it difficult to know what he could say, except that there was no evidence upon which a jury could convict.' The result was that there was still only a minimal amount of detail known for sure about the scene of the crime. All it came down to was that there had been a savage and merciless assault and murder, and then the body had been put in a pose that suggested some kind of sexual attack.

Finally, we have to consider Harry Ramshaw. The man said that he went into the dock with a clear conscience. A reporter from the *Evening Telegraph* went with the news of the acquittal to his sister-in-law, Mrs Herbert Ramshaw, who lived in Newland Drive in Scunthorpe, and also to his sister in Hull, Ida. The whole family had been through a traumatic time, and had all been convinced that he was innocent.

Harry's brother, Herbert, travelled back to Scunthorpe with him, on a bus. It would have been a long, slow journey. They came home to a celebratory afternoon tea. His sister made a statement to the press: 'We never believed he was guilty, and his workmates and friends who had known him for years have said they would not believe it either, of a man like him.'

In the end, we have to look on the behaviour of the detectives with extreme suspicion and a certain amount of revulsion. What actually went on in the two interrogations will never be known, but all available opinions and reports suggest that the actions taken were grossly unfair when they were dealing with a man of Harry Ramshaw's nature. There is a photograph that gives a triumphant closure to the saga of the Charlesworth case: it shows Harry with his brother and sister, smiling, as they sit together. In the picture, Harry is a small, quiet man; nothing suggests that he has been through hell, but that is not overstating the situation. We can only guess at what feelings were going through him as he was subjected to the pressure of a 'grilling.' With hindsight, it is impossible to see why the investigation took the rather sinister turn it did when the detectives decided that some pressure applied would resolve things; it was a dangerous risk.

The case remains in one of the unsolved categories in the chronicles of Lincolnshire crime. Whoever the 'homicidal maniac' was, he was never traced. The entire unpleasant story of how Emily Charlesworth died has to be consigned to that number of cases in which a suspect had to be found and the consequences were disastrous. From start to finish, the murder case had been highly sensational and shrouded in mystery; the way it was reported provides an exemplar for the terrifying power of media amplification, as the town thought there was a madman loose, and that the 'beer bottle' clue made any suspicious character in any one of the dozen town-centre pubs immediately frightening to the ordinary folk. The local press had reported the whole narrative of the killing and the hunt with astounding verve and enthusiasm; they reported well and accurately, but the spin-off was likely to exacerbate the increasingly apprehensive atmosphere in the town, although great emphasis was placed on the likelihood that the 'maniac' had most likely left town. It must make this tale one of the most ironical in this respect; that so many rough and desperate characters were around the steel town at this time, and yet a harmless, child-like man was pulled in and charged, a man who never went out for a night of heavy drinking, who cared for his dearest friend and was cared for by her, and who worked hard in tough conditions. Justice was done in the end, and was patently seen to be done.

The Emily Charlesworth case has to go down as one of the three most prominent Scunthorpe unsolved murders of the last century. The other investigations had a fair amount of technology to back them up, and more sophisticated police strategies; the Charlesworth investigation was one in which blinkers were put on by the police team and some very obvious obstacles were overlooked. Regarding the nature of the interviews with Ramshaw, we will never know the truth, but one ironical comment must be made. In the *Report of the Departmental Committee on Detective Work and Procedure* (1938) there is only one sentence concerning interviews with suspects in the main chapters; emphasis in this is on crime records, procedure, liaison and so on. The one reference to interviewing is this, 'that a man who has completed the course should have a good knowledge of criminal law and of court procedure, and what is more important, should have demonstrated to him and have learned sound and systematic methods in the examination of a scene of crime, the questioning of witnesses ...' One wonders what kind of skills were imparted to the officers in this case.

Epilogue: Paranormal?

The accounts of trials and investigations here have all been concerned with the process of law. But what about that element which figures so often in memoirs and journalism – the place of chance or indeed of the unexplained, the paranormal? This anecdote from a writer back in the 1920s illustrates how, at times, the boundaries between normal and bizarre experience cross.

The tale is told by Henry Spicer, a writer who, in 1920, described how a Cambridge scholar was staying in Exeter, doing some study in a peaceful place near to the ferry which crossed at that time to the Starcross station of the Great Western Railway. At midnight one day, while he was reading in bed, a mysterious voice told him, 'Go down to the ferry.' He thought his tired mind was making this up, or that he was in the borderland between sleeping and being awake, so he ignored it, but it spoke again. It said, 'The boatman waits.' He considered what to do, and eventually decided that this was something extraordinary, so he decided he would walk to the ferry, out of mere curiosity.

The boatman said he had been expecting him. The scholar was now thoroughly perplexed. It emerged that the boatman had also heard a voice, telling him to ferry the scholar across the river. When they had crossed the river the scholar just knew that he had to go into Exeter, and he did so. When he arrived there, he went for some breakfast and had to wait. The waiter said he was sorry for the slow service but the place was buzzing with the sensation of the murder trial taking place at the assizes in town. Spicer wrote: 'Upon the whole, the man's volubility ended by inspiring the young scholar D.... with a portion of his own interest in the matter and accordingly he strolled about until the court opened ...'

In court, there was a man in the dock who was a carpenter, and he said that he could not have done the murder, that he had an alibi, and that if he could only find the gentleman who was with him when he was doing a job of work on the day of the crime he would be exonerated. The scholar took a closer look; he thought for a moment, and then he remembered meeting the man – it was at a friend's house, and the scholar had taken out his notebook and he had lost his pencil. The carpenter had given him his own pencil, and that had been used.

Spicer concluded the tale with the detail that the scholar had the same notebook on him as he sat in court; he took it out, and there was the very note he had written that day, using the carpenter's pencil.

The scholar gave testimony and the accused man walked away free.

Conclusions

Escapes from the noose have been varied and complex in the process of events from trial or conviction to freedom or commutation. Over the centuries, the gradual diminution in the scale and number of capital offences has been marked by certain watersheds such as the Peel ministry or the 1861 Offences Against the Persons Act. The twentieth century campaigns for the abolition of hanging is markedly significant and was successful in forcing a sequence of legislation to change things, notably the views on diminished responsibility and insanity. Yet if we look back to earlier centuries, it is astonishing to note just how much there was in the criminal justice systems of past regimes that depended on whimsicality, circumstances and error in these matters.

For the historian, arguably the period of greatest interest in respect of reprieves and respites was the Regency. In those years, the Home Office matured and its status and function was defined in this context. In that age of sedition and paranoia, with the ancient regime across the English Channel showing how fragile the stability of a government was in the face of rebellion, hanging and transportation were accelerated at first, with plenty of instances of multiple hangings. The eighteenth century murder acts and the 'bloody code' meant that repression and fear were the weapons of repression. Looking for humane attitudes at the time might seem to be a strange occupation, but I hope I have shown that in fact, there were plenty of ways in which local factors, human empathy and sheer pity played a part.

The notion of a pardon has always added the dimension of absolute drama and paranoia to prison regimes. On the wall of one prison, when I visited in 2004, there was still a photocopy of a royal pardon fixed to a notice board. That document is just one of many which still resonate down the years when we think of people in the condemned cell waiting for a letter from the Home Secretary and a knock on the cell door from the Governor – up to the very last moment of life.

The appeal courts after 1907 become places of drama too: the ritual or procedure, dress code, positions within the court furniture, esoteric and forbidding language, all played a part in the shock and fascination of those theatres of fear and expectancy. There may have been high tragedy there, but one suspects that more often it was a case of total abject terror for the accused. The barristers must surely have felt a tremor of deep anxiety beneath the wig and gown of their office.

In England, all this ended with the Act abolishing capital punishment in 1964. In the Channel Islands and in the Isle of Man, there were still death sentences, even as late as the 1990s, but none were carried out.

Sources and Bibliography

Primary Sources: Books and Monographs

Ballantine, Mr Serjeant *Some Experiences of a Barrister's Life* (Bentley, London, 1883)

Birkett, Lord *Six Great Advocates* (Penguin, London, 1961)

Report of an Enquiry into the Confession made by David John Ware of the Murder of Olive Balchin (HMSO, 1947)

Criminal Appeal: Court Records (Annual, Sweet and Maxwell, to 1966)

Humphreys, Travers *Criminal Days* (Hodder and Stoughton, London, 1946)

Secondary Sources: Books

Annual Register various years, collected volumes, publishers; Baldwin, Craddock and Joy

Anon. *Fifty Amazing Hairbreadth Escapes* (Odhams, London, 1920)

Birkenhead, Earl of *More Famous Trials* (Hutchinson, London, 1910)

Bresler, Fenton *Reprieve: A Study of a System* (Harrap, London, 1968)

Browne, Douglas G. and Tullett, E. V. *Bernard Spilsbury: his life and cases* (Harrap, London, 1951)

Campbell, Jimmy Powdrell *A Scottish Murder* (Tempus, 2007)

Deans, R. Storry *Notable Trials: romances of the law courts* (Cassell, London, 1896)

Denning, Lord *Landmarks of the Law* (Butterworths, London, 1984)

Eddleston, John J. *The Encyclopaedia of Executions* (Blake, London, 2002)

Emsley, Clive *Crime and Society in England 1750-1900* (Pearson, Harlow, 1996)

Hale, Leslie *Hanged in Error* Penguin Special (Penguin, London, 1961)

Jackson, Robert *The Chief: the biography of Gordon Hewart, Lord Chief Justice of England 1922-40* (Harrap, London, 1959)

Jackson, Robert *Francis Camps: famous case histories of the most celebrated pathologist of our time* (Granada, London, 1983)

Lane, Brian *The Encyclopaedia of Forensic Science* (Headline, London, 1982)

Linebaugh, Peter *The London Hanged* (Verso, London, 2003)

Marjoribanks, Edward *The Life of Sir Edward Marshall Hall* (Gollancz, London, 1929)

Priestley, Philip *Victorian Prison Lives* (Pimlico, London, 1995)

Rolph, C. H. *The Queen's Pardon* (Cassell, London, 1978)

Roughead, William *Tales of the Criminous* (Cassell, London, 1956)

Woodley, Mick *Osborn's Concise Law Dictionary* (Sweet and Maxwell, London, 2005)

Periodicals

The Illustrated London News
History Today
Journal of the Police History Society
Legal History
Police Journal
Social History
Punch

Web Sources and Digital

The Times Digital Archive
www.murderfiles.com
See The Ultimate Price: the unlawful killing of English Police Officers (CD)

Index